The Future of Germanistik

© 1996
Department of Germanic and Slavic Languages
Vanderbilt University

Distributed by Vanderbilt University Press

A DAAD-Sponsored Symposium at Vanderbilt University
October 13–16, 1994

The publication of this volume was made possible by the generous
support of the German Academic Exchange Service in New York and
the University Research Council at Vanderbilt University.

Manufactured in the United States of America

Library of Congress Cataloguing-in-Publication Data

The Future of Germanistik in the USA: changing our prospects / edited by John A.
  McCarthy and Katrin Schneider.
     p.   cm.
  "A DAAD-sponsored symposium at Vanderbilt University, October 13–16,
  1994"—t.p.verso.
  Includes bibliographical references.
  ISBN 0-8265-1281-X (paper)
     1. German philology—Study and teaching—United States—Congresses.
  2. German philology—Study and teaching (Higher)—United States—
  Congresses. 3. Germanists—United States—Congresses. I. McCarthy, John A.
  (John Aloysius), 1942– II. Schneider, Katrin, 1967–
     PF3068.U6F88 1996
438'.007'073—dc20   95-50037

THE FUTURE OF GERMANISTIK IN THE USA

Changing Our Prospects

Edited by
John A. McCarthy
and
Katrin Schneider

Department of Germanic and Slavic Languages
Vanderbilt University
Distributed by
Vanderbilt University Press

CONTENTS

Part II: Curriculum Matters

Part III: (Re)Shaping the Discipline

IV: Concluding Remarks

PREFACE

Despite all the attention accorded it, the role of German in the American Academy continues to be a source of fascination, even of consternation. Is there a need for reform? Is reform possible? Is the practice of Germanistik in the USA American enough? Is it "at home" in North America?

Notable products of earlier endeavors to address these concerns include the volumes *German Studies in the United States: Assessment and Outlook* (1976) edited by Walter F. W. Lohnes & Valters Nollendorfs; *Teaching German in America: Prolegomena to a History* (1988) again edited by Lohnes & Nollendorfs joined by David Benseler. In 1989 Frank Trommler edited an anthology, *Germanistik in den USA. Neue Entwicklungen und Methoden* (1989), the same year that the special issue of *The German Quarterly*, 62.2 (1989) on *Germanistik as German Studies: Interdisciplinary Theories and Methods* appeared. Each endeavor represents an effort to widen the circle of issues which should be of concern to teachers and professors of German across the nation, whether it is a matter of writing the history of the study of German in America, the significance of new developments in the realm of theory, or plotting a course to ensure the future of the profession. More recently the discussions have been enriched by the graduate-student generated volume on *Rethinking Germanistik* (1991), designed to revitalize and expand the German canon taught in the USA, and a special number of *Weimarer Beiträge* devoted to explaining the American situation to a German audience entitled simply, *Germanistik in den USA* (1993). The culminating work in this procession is John Van Cleve and A. Leslie Willson's polemical *Remarks on the Needed Reform of German Studies in the United States* (1993) which proved to be the last straw. As exhaustive as this list appears to be, it is by no means complete.

While American Germanists have been busy rethinking their profession and reflecting upon their very *raison d'être*, German Germanists have not been twiddling their thumbs either. They have had their parallel discussions which have become increasingly intense and iconoclastic. In 1967 such noteworthy Germanists as Eberhard Lämmert, Walther Killy, and Karl Otto Conrady published papers in a volume entitled *Germanistik - Eine Deutsche Wissenschaft* (1967). The discussion was expanded two years later with *Ansichten einer künftigen Germanistik* (1969) edited by Jürgen Kolbe and a third volume of essays, *Neue Ansichten einer künftigen Germanistik* (1974), also edited by Kolbe. The debate is renewed more recently by such publications as *Wozu noch Germanistik? Wissenschaft, Beruf, Kulturelle Praxis* (1989) edited by Jürgen Förster, Eva Neuland, & Gerhard Rupp; Peter Zimmermann's (ed.) *Interkulturelle Germanistik: Dialog der Kulturen auf Deutsch?* (1991), and Eitel Timm's (ed.) *Challenges of Germanistik: Traditions and Prospects of an Academic Discipline = Germanistik Weltweit?: Zur Theorie und Praxis des Disziplinrahmens* (1992).

These titles are cited so extensively, not to bore you, but to underscore a point. Yes, the debate on the nature, even the survivability of Germanistik on both sides of the Atlantic has been going on for some time now and in parallel fashion. The American publications have been rather consistent: each one talks about the need for reform, i.e. to become more "American." The Germans have evolved in a remarkable way. Beginning with a simple, classically sculpted title emphasizing that Germanistik is a specifically German discipline, the debate feeds into the essay collections by Zimmermann and Timm with their emphasis on the German perspective within an "interkultureller Germanistik." Timm chose a distinctly contorted and macaronic title which seems to promise Germanistik as a world-wide phenomenon. No doubt about it. Germanics is in a crisis: "hüben und drüben."

Thus, the essays in this volume are part and parcel of an ongoing debate concerning the proper role for Germanics in the USA. A number of questions served as guidelines in the planning of the Vanderbilt symposium. Does our continuing crisis have anything to do with the continued tendency in some quarters to fill tenured positions in our German departments with German bred and trained Germanists when there has been no lack of native talent? Does it have anything to do with the continued tendency of some graduate departments to recruit Ph.D. candidates from German universities? Does it have anything to do with the still dominant tendency to conduct our business in German, a policy seemingly ill designed to catch the attention of sponsoring institutions, reach a broader public, or make us a visible and viable force on campus and within our communities? Are we satisfied that the DAAD, the Goethe Institute, and the Austrian Institute will be there with open pocket books always at the ready to support our efforts? Ultimately, we are asking how "American" has the curriculum become?

An immediate catalyst for the Vanderbilt symposium on the future of Germanics in the USA was Van Cleve and Willson's *Remarks on the Needed Reform of German Studies in the United States*. The Vanderbilt meeting can in fact be viewed as a response to their call for a series of debates on all aspects of the ongoing crisis in the profession. While itself a strange mixture of vitriolic diatribe and keen insight, their book succeeds in stimulating debate. The authors designate an agenda for the next decade and suggest that the overall goal should be to raise the enrollment in German to 200,000 students by the year 2002, thereby reaching the enrollment level of 1968 before the most recent decline. The authors envision a national agenda, that is, one that will benefit Germanists whether they live and work in Philadelphia, Madison, Eugene, or Oxford, Mississippi. They perceive in the profession a pervasive sense of inertia and a lack of unified direction. They are concerned that the profession has not adequately addressed the issue of declining enrollments in German for the past 25 years and that Germanists remain largely invisible on our campuses. Ultimately, they call for a candid and broad reevaluation of our profession against the backdrop of the history of our response to the mounting crisis over the past twenty-five years. Those responses include GDR literature, German-American studies, culture studies, business German, women studies, film studies, and alternate careers.[1] Have they worked? Is the profession better off as a result?

These points are worthy of consideration. One must say to the authors' credit that they do acknowledge their reflections to be a

---

[1] Cf. also *Rethinking "Germanistik": Canon and Culture*, ed. by Robert Bledsoe, Bernd Estabrook, J. Courtney Federle, Kay Henschel, Wayne Miller, and Arnim Polster (New York: Peter Lang, 1991) and *"Interkulturelle Germanistik". Dialog der Kulturen auf Deutsch!*, ed. Peter Zimmermann, 2nd rev. ed. (Frankfurt a/M: Peter Lang, 1991).

polemic, seeing their assault as a necessary "means of breaking through the inertia that afflicts American Germanics, an inertia so pervasive that we have had to proceed on the assumption that it affects even the well-disposed reader."[2] Whether one agrees or not that it is salutary to speak publicly about perceived problems (real or not), we certainly all agree that it is important to speak freely about what moves some to go public with (private) concerns. And surely, no one can fault Van Cleve and Willson for wanting to raise expectations for our field (57). This present volume represents an attempt to go public with "private" concerns.

Striking about the Van Cleve/Willson volume is its aggressive tone, as if the authors had lost patience with a colossus which refuses to budge. Given their perception that Germanics is "sliding silently toward oblivion," their frantic call to arms is understandable. Their primary hope was to initiate a dialogue on the future of the profession. What they downplay is that a vigorous debate had been going on for two generations before their book appeared. The organizers of the Vanderbilt conference agree, however, that "the crisis in American Germanics will abate only after meetings, debates, resolutions, more meetings - and finally, joint action" (ix).

The premise, however, is not new. It was first formulated in emphatic fashion 20 years ago in 1976 in the volume, *German Studies in the United States: Assessment and Outlook*. Like Van Cleve and Willson, Lohnes and Nollendorfs remark that their volume is intended to engender critical reflection on our profession. They also decried the strong identification of American Germanics with German *Germanistik* and outlined various ways in which we differ from them. Moreover, they hoped to establish a professional network as a means of advancing the reform of Germanics from within.

Many of us were just launching our careers when that call to critical self-reflection and reform was sounded. Some of us issued that call back then. Where are we now? What has happened to the promise of a gradual Americanization of our field through the "combination of constricted employment opportunities and current immigration regu-

---

[2] John Van Cleve and A. Leslie Willson, *Remarks on the Needed Reform of German Studies in the United States* (Columbia SC: Camden House, 1993), 81.

lations" predicted by Jeffrey Sammons back then?[3] As late as 1988 Henry J. Schmidt engaged in a mental game of determining who readily comes to mind as leading figures in the field of Germanics. 75% of the top 12 persons were native speakers of German; of the top 24, 71% were native-German speakers, and of the top 100 most active members of the profession 60% had a German background.[4] Schmidt's calculations were admittedly subjective, so we should take them with a grain of salt. Yet there are some departments where three-fourths of the full-time German faculty are native speakers. In one, four of five recent positions were filled with native speakers. But then that experience might be nothing more than an anomaly. Still we need to speak about it, given the profession's history of being a discipline of immigrants.

In many ways, this conference should not even have been necessary; moreover, not all those colleagues who should have been there were in fact there. The list of participants represents only a fraction of those qualified to reexamine the role of Germanics in the American Academy. Practical considerations like the size of the budget and the size of the room dictated in part who could be present. The conferees were, therefore, conscious of being just a part of a much larger whole. The intent of the symposium was - in good American fashion - to focus attention on practical strategies to manage our natural resources in German in a more efficient and productive manner. To this end, a possible action agenda for the profession to ensure our vigor for the twenty-first century was the last item of business.

To reach that goal a series of position papers where offered to stimulate uninhibited discussion of key issues: our professional profile, our visibility in the academy, the configuration of the undergraduate and graduate curricula, the role of multiperspectivism and cultural studies, and the shaping of the profession through our journals and

---

[3] Jeffrey Sammons, "Some Considerations on Our Invisibility," in *German Studies in the United States: Assessment and Outlook* (Madison WI: U of Wisconsin P, 1976), 22.

[4] Henry J. Schmidt, "Wissenschaft als Ware und als Selbstbehauptung. Die institutionellen Grundlagen der amerikanischen Germanistik," in *Germanistik in den USA - Neue Entwicklungen und Methoden*, ed. by Frank Trommler (Opladen: Westdeutscher Verlag, 1989), 71.

publishing activities (a panel discussion). Colleagues were enlisted as respondents or panelists or moderators. Regardless of the role, each person contributed to animated and open debate. The recommended readings announced ahead of time (see the bibliography) were intended to provide a common basis of discourse, augmenting the individual, subjective perspectives. Our purpose was not to prescribe a course of action or to be inflexible in pursuing a particular direction for the future. On the contrary, we wished to explore multiple perspectives and hopefully enhance our sensibilities in order to be more effective members of the profession.

The participants in the symposium agreed that selected presentations and responses be made available as quickly as possible in published form in the hope that the vigorous discussion of critical issues facing the profession of Germanics in the USA might reach a wider audience. The candor and tone of the original presentations have been preserved in order to convey a sense of the immediacy felt at the symposium itself. What could not be captured was the intensity of the discussions which these presentations occasioned. In order to convey a sense of the interaction characteristic of the meeting, however, four participants were invited to compose a brief response from their particular perspective as silent observer, outsider to the profession, novice, and organizer. They are included in the final section of this volume labelled "Concluding Remarks." Two additional papers are included, although they were not officially presented at the symposium (those by Nollendorfs and Natter) because they succinctly summarize freqently addressed issues in the symposium deliberations. If this volume contributes to a sharper focus on our problems and their practical solutions, then the ultimate objective of the symposium will have been realized.

This symposium was made possible through the generous support of the German Academic Exchange Service (DAAD), the University of Delaware, and Vanderbilt University. A Special note of thanks is due Dr. Heidrun Suhr, then Director of the DAAD, Chancellor Joe B. Wyatt, Provost Thomas Burish, Arts and Science Dean Madeleine J. Goodman, Graduate School Dean Russell G. Hamilton, and Alice C. Harris, Chair of the Department of Germanic & Slavic Languages - all of Vanderbilt University - for their personal involvement as well as monetary support. A special note of gratitude is also due Gottfried

Gügold of the DAAD NY for his part in making this volume possible through a generous publication subsidy. The University Research Council of Vanderbilt University provided a grant to support the production of the volume. Without that level of subvention, the volume could not be so attractively priced.

John A. McCarthy
October 1995

1

Double Optics:
The Americanization of Germanistik—
The Germanization of Americans

JOHN A. MCCARTHY
Vanderbilt University

In the introduction to his *Gregorius*, Hartmann von Aue warned his audience that the tale they were about to hear would not be entirely to their liking. They might feel non-plussed, maybe morally offended, or at the very least discomfitted by a socially taboo topic. Like Hartmann's radical departure from courtly mores, my own questioning of latent predispositions, even incestuousness, underlying our professional practices might strike you as being "vil starc ze hoerenne"! Far from wishing to cause discomfit for its own sake, however, I am really interested in opening up the debate on the issues facing our profession to a broad diversity of voices and perspectives. Inclusion is the operative word here, not exclusion. Above all, I am not interested in "business as usual." However, candor in addressing publicly taboo topics is prerequisite to finding practical solutions to the very real problems besetting the profession.

The title of these opening remarks is a direct allusion to a suggestion made by Jeffrey Sammons a few years ago in his essay, "Germanistik in Niemandsland," to develop a double optics in the pursuit of our disciplinary objectives. He uses "double optics" to refer to a dual focus on our own intellectual and cultural environment in the USA as well as on the tensions between German culture and American culture which shape our professional identity. His

1

hope is that this kind of "double optics" will act in a modest way as a bridge across the cultural divide between the two societies. Sammons wrote in 1989: "Zu entwickeln wäre eine doppelte Optik, einmal auf die eigene geisteswissenschaftliche und kulturelle Umgebung, dann auf das Auseinanderstreben unserer beiden Kulturen gerichtet, um es bewußt zu machen und ihm sogar vielleicht in bescheidenem Grade entgegenzuwirken."[1]

The question of double optics is also central to Marilyn Sibley Fries's remarks on the role of women in Germanistik both as writers and purveyors of German literature. Despite obvious gains in the last ten years, she still considers our discipline to be a man's domain and senses that women engaged in feminist scholarship appear as a threat to the male way of doing Germanistik. This is the primary reason why she recommends a psychoanalytical approach to the study of American Germanistik, for it would prove fruitful in laying bare variations of a double optics. Marilyn wrote in 1993: "Die Versuchung liegt nahe, eine Psychoanalyse der amerikanischen Germanistik zu unternehmen, bei der unter anderem die Verhältnisse zwischen Männern und Frauen, Deutschen und Amerikanern sowie den verschiedenen Generationen untersucht werden müßten."[2] The problems with which women have to contend in terms of who determines their hiring, tenure, and promotion, is similar to the configuration of forces which determine the hiring and promotion of nonnative speakers. Dealing with such double optics lies at the center of my own reflections on the state of and future prospects for our profession.

Let me state my actual conclusion at the outset for fear that you

[1] Jeffrey Sammons, "Germanistik in Niemandsland," in *Germanistik in den USA: Neue Entwicklungen und Methoden*, ed. by Frank Trommler (Opladen: Westdeutscher Verlag, 1989), 104-20; here 118. Whereas Sammons has in mind a dual perspective on American culture and its difference from German culture in our hermeneutic encounters with the German, I would argue that "eine doppelte Optik" should include the full utilization of our natural resources in a discipline still heavily indebted to immigrant managers.

[2] Marilyn Sibley Fries, "Rezeption deutschsprachiger Autorinnen in den USA," *Weimarer Beiträge* 39.3 (1993): 410-46. Biddy Martin, "Zwischenbilanz der feministischen Debatten, in *Germanistik in den USA* (1989), 165-95, offers an overview of feminist theory as it impacts upon German Studies in North America.

may not be as attentive toward the end of my remarks as you are at their beginning: Unless we respond in pragmatic fashion to the double optics operative on several levels of our professional life and acknowledge openly the tacit goals of the profession of German in the United States, we have little hope of truly altering the profile of our profession or of significantly improving our prospects for the future. On-going efforts to make Germanistik "more American" will not succeed.[3] Germanics will remain eurocentric and marginalized. North Americans will continue to be remade in the likeness of their German mentors or they simply will not be able to compete in a tight marketplace.

My observations are informed by my own personal perspective, for I am what John Van Cleve and A. Leslie Willson call a "wannabe"; that is, a non-native speaker who is driven to be just like the Germans who have mentored him or her in the discipline of Germanistik. Being a wannabe has been good for me; but increasingly I wonder how good it has been for the profession. For example, an essay of mine recently appeared in a North American journal on a major American writer, Ralph Waldo Emerson. I composed the piece in German; I aimed it at a German-speaking audience. But I published it in America. The sudden realization of the absurdity of my intent gave me pause to think about my role as an American Germanist and what responsibility I have for making Germanist scholarship readily available to colleagues in English and American literature. Those colleagues not infrequently view us as being cliquish because of our insistence upon using German as our language of communication ... even when we have something of direct interest to say to them. Perhaps I have unwittingly contributed all these years to the problems confronting us now.

Time and time again since the 1960s it has been observed that Germanistik in the United States is a discipline in crisis. Its history can even be interpreted, as Peter Uwe Hohendahl suggests, as "a

---

[3] See Valters Nollendorfs, "Eine amerikanischere Germanistik. Entwicklungen im amerikanischen Deutschstudium in den 70er und 80er Jahren," *Zeitschrift für Kulturaustausch* 35 (1985): 230-36.

series of (failed) attempts to solve [that] crisis.[4] One of the most recent assessments, "Out of *Germanistik*: Thoughts on the Shape of Things to Come" by Valters Nollendorfs, contains for me an unwitting double-entendre; when I read "out of Germanistik" I immediately thought of "out of gas." And I began to muse: where do we go to from here?[5]

Germanics in America is essentially without a home and without an identity, for it exists—to adopt Sammons' oft-quoted formulation—in a "no-man's land" and is isolated from its sister disciplines.[6] When the first European settlers came to America they considered the continent to be a no-man's land and began to lay claim to it, dislodging native Americans from their traditional territories. Subsequent waves of immigrants brought their culture(s) with them to fill the vast cultural void between the Atlantic and the Pacific. European map makers established a set of coordinates by means of which they could navigate the vast uncharted terrain. Those coordinates proved to be quite similar to those of central European nations. For many newcomers America remains a cultural no-man's land. In this no-man's land no one seems to take note of American Germanics. Even though ours is a very active and productive discipline, it seems falsely placed.[7] On the other hand, how much notice

---

[4] Peter U. Hohendahl, "Interdisciplinary German Studies: Tentative Conclusions," *The German Quarterly* 62.2 (Spring 1989): 227-34, here 227.

[5] Valters Nollendorfs, "Out of *Germanistik*: Thoughts on the Shape of Things to Come," *Die Unterrichtspraxis* 27.1 (spring 1994): 1-10.

[6] Sammons, "Germanistik in Niemandsland," in *Germanistik in den USA*, Sammons attributes the "homelessness" of Germanics in the States to wider conditions of cultural miscommunication (cf. 115). See also Frank Trommler, "Einleitung," in *Germanistik in den USA*, 19. Trommler summarizes the motif of the absence of a self-image for American Germanics, citing as its causes the pluralism of methodologies and the selective reception of individual American Germanists in Germany. Willi Goetschel repeats the association of no-man's land as being a methodological hodgepodge but welcomes the shift toward German Studies. See W. G., "Zu diesem Heft: Germanistik in den USA," *Weimarer Beiträge* 39.3 (1993): 331-32.

[7] Wulf Koepke, "Germanistik als eine deutsch-amerikanische Wissenschaft," in *Germanistik in den USA*, describes the discipline as it was 20 years ago ... and as it still is: "die Germanistik [sah] wie ein zwar sehr aktives, aber eigentlich nutzloses und falsch plaziertes Fach [aus]."61.

do *we* take of *our* own environment?[8] Are we merely situated or can we be actively situating?[9] How responsive have we actually been to the cultural and intellectual context of North America? It is high time that we rechart the cultural and intellectual landscape so that we will be better situated as contributing members to American academia and society at large.[10]

While the nature of our crisis bears some similarity to the crisis of Germanistik in the fatherland in that both entail a radical questioning of disciplinary identity and purpose, there are fundamental differences. German Germanistik came under attack in the late 1960s as a useless, socially unengaged discipline, a stance captured poignantly in the catch-phrase: "Schlagt die Germanistik tot, macht die blaue Blume rot!" The hopes and aspirations for a "zukünftige Germanistik" led to some significant changes but not necessarily to its revitalization. The current expression of a "Krisenlarmoyanz," the hopes for a "Dynamisierungschance," and the calls for an ever "zukünftigere Germanistik" sound very much like what American Germanics is experiencing in its own search for "disciplinary identity" and "cultural contribution."[11] Yet the crisis on that side of the

---

[8] Henry J. Schmidt, "Wissenschaft als Ware und als Selbstbehauptung. Die institutionellen Grundlagen der amerikanischen Germanistik," in *Germanistik in Amerika*, writes, for example: "Zudem klagt man, daß die Außenwelt wenig von der amerikanischen Germanistik wahrnimmt. Was aber—um den Spieß umzudrehen—nimmt sie von der Außenwelt wahr?" (80).

[9] John McCumber draws this distinction with regard to the function of reason in a traditional and a postmodern sense. The traditional role of reason is to accept its position and define its environment from that fixed point. Situating reason, on the other hand, is dynamic, moving from period center to period center, thereby enriching its insights through changing perspectives. See John McCumber, *Poetic Interaction: Language, Freedom, Reason* (Chicago: U of Chicago P, 1989), 374-75.

[10] One of the most vocal advocates of recharting the course of German departments has been Jeffrey M. Peck. See, e.g., his "'The British are coming! The British are coming!' Notes for a Comparative Study of Institutions," in *Teaching German in America: Prolegomena to a History*, ed. by David P. Benseler, Walter F. W. Lohnes, and Valters Nollendorfs (Madison WI: U of Wisconsin P, 1988), 271-84.

[11] See the various reactions by Friedmar Apel, Klaus Weimar, Thomas Steinfeld, Heinz Schlaffer, and Friedrich Kittler to the *Germanistentag* in Aachen, "Germanistik—disziplinäre Identität und kulturelle Leistung," as reported in the *Frankfurter Allgemeine Zeitung*, Mittwoch, 7. September 1994, Nr. 208, Seite N5.

Atlantic is not the same as on our side. We are not a "staatlich appro-
bierte und finanzierte Organisation" (Klaus Weimar) nor can we
count on German being taught in the schools as a legitimation of our
existence at the post-secondary level. Our existential dilemma plays
itself out in the cultural divide between Germans and Americans. We
enjoy no privileged position.

The problem, as oft diagnosed (mostly by language methodolo-
gists rather than by proponents of German Studies), is that
Germanists in the States have a two-fold mission: one is to teach
German as a foreign language to students who frequently fail to grasp
the importance of multilingualism; the second is to engage in intellectually stimulating, methodologically sound scholarship of the
highest quality worthy of recognition (by colleagues abroad!).
Teaching German as a second language, however, is not a source of
disciplinary identity in our graduate schools, while rigorous scholarship on literary and intellectual matters is (Nollendorfs 1994: 5A).
The first is sometimes even viewed ahistorically as being a "prostitu-
tion" of our metier.[12] To achieve the first objective we must narrow
the distance separating American culture from German culture. To
achieve the second goal we have frequently endeavored to clone
German scholarship (and German scholars) in America.

The bifocality of language instruction on the one hand and intellectual rigor on the other has split the personality of American
Germanists. Language instructor, textbook writer, and language-
acquisition specialist remain distant cousins of the graduate professor.[13] An American Germanist who endeavors to accomplish both
tasks is exposed to unhealthy tensions. A divided self cannot stand.
The double optics of language teacher and seminar leader has con-

---

[12] Peter Höyng, "Zur 'Krise' der Germanistik in den USA," *Zeitschrift für
Literaturwissenschaft und Linguistik* 97 (1995): 164. On the other hand, Höyng is right
to see an important source of the crisis to reside outside the discipline of Germanistik
itself in a general loss of interest in literature as a value in its own right, although I
hesitate to see that "Funktionsverlust" as "der 'eigentliche' Kern der Krise" (165). The
sources of our crisis are multiple.

[13] David P. Benseler, "The Upper-Division Curriculum in Foreign Languages and
Literatures: Obstacles to the Realization of Promise," in *Critical Issues in Foreign
Language Instruction,* ed. Ellen S. Silber (New York: Garland, 1991), 186-99, draws
attention to a major oversight due to this divided professorate. The upper-division curriculum rightfully represents for him unexplored terrain.

fused, I suggest, the Germanization of Americans with the Americanization of Germanics. We have not made Germanistik more American by making Americans more German.

Nor is Germanics more American because native speakers of German practice it in America. Mere physical presence in the States is no guarantee for a mentality change. I do not necessarily see, therefore, "an inevitable trend" toward the Americanization of the profession as Nollendorfs does simply because "starting with those [colleagues] born in the 1940s, the native North Americans constitute the absolute majority in German departments" (1994: 7). While there is evidence of demographic change, hiring and promotion decisions still proceed too often according to the old biases. Native speakers born before 1945 still dominate policy decisions in many departments. The title of these opening remarks, "Double Optics," refers then also to the double bind which has characterized German in the American Academy ever since the late 1960s. It is the world as I know it.

Yet the problem outlined here is by no means homogeneous. Being responsive to our North-American environment is something language teachers must do in order to survive. We must compete with other language departments for students or go under. Language instruction has become savvy, up-to-date, and ultimately market-driven. Germanistik proper and German Studies, the other personality within our schizophrenic beings, have been less successful not because of a lack of effort and innovative ideas (especially in German Studies), but because of the intransigence of the structure of departments and of institutions themselves. Maybe also because of the dissolution of a focus on literary studies. I am not sure.

In any event, to break out of their intellectual isolation, German departments have moved toward German Studies, incorporating into the curriculum courses on New German Cinema, the holocaust, philosophy and literature, history and literary theory, feminist perspectives and critical theory.[14] Outwardly, we have seemingly come a

---

[14] For an overview of these developments see Heidrun Suhr, "German Studies in North America: Contexts and Perspectives," in *Präludien. Kanadisch-Deutsche Dialoge*, ed. Burkhardt Krause, Ulrich Scheck, and Patrick O'Neill (München: Judicium Verlag, 1992), 105-119.

long way from the first calls for reform issued from such places as Madison, Wisconsin, in the 1970s. Many of us have come to view Germanics as part of a larger whole which it in part must reflect (Koepke 1989: 63). Now the call has been issued for "German Across the Curriculum," taking German out of the German department and putting it in any classroom that makes sense. We can't help but greet this move with enthusiasm, although one might shudder to hear a simultaneous call to hire more native speakers across the curriculum.

There is to my mind, however, a deep-seated, persistent problem which must be solved before Germanistik in the USA can achieve full integration in the intellectual and cultural life of America. The problem has to do with the Germans and with the self-identity of Americans. As early as 1976 Victor Lange lamented the lack of "independence of judgment ... in American academic studies of German," chiding teachers of German for not recognizing the need to address an American audience in its professional activities.[15] Historically Germanistik in the United States has been what Wulf Koepke calls an "Einwandererwissenschaft" (Koepke 1989: 63), beginning with the Forty-Eighters and continuing to this day. He contends: "Die starke Beeinflussung durch neue Einwanderer hat einerseits zu hohem akademischen Niveau geführt, andererseits die Verwurzelung der Disziplin in den USA behindert" (64). When he wrote that in 1988 Koepke was confident that the wave of emigrants was gradually subsiding and that the way would open up for the fuller integration of Germanics in the larger North-American context. It will be fascinating, he concluded, to see how the new relationship between the German "Nachkriegseinwanderer" and their American "Schüler" will work itself out (64). Four years later Willi Goetschel remarked positively upon the influx of new talent from Europe which has so enriched Germanics in several different waves of immigration and from which we continue to "profit" today.[16]

---

[15] Victor Lange, "Thoughts in Season," in *German Studies in the United States: Assessment and Outlook*, by Walter F. W. Lohnes and Valters Nollendorfs (U of Wisconsin P, 1976), 12-13.

[16] Willi Goetschel, *Weimarer Beiträge* 39.3 (1993), 331. In citing this continued

Surely, I am not alone in wincing at the implication of these statements that intellectual rigor in American Germanics is due to the presence of the Europeans and that the Americans will succeed by becoming "disciples" of their European mentors. Unfortunately, there are signs that importations into the (restricted) marketplace of the American Academy refuse to subside: e.g., Wisconsin, Columbia, NYU, Penn State and Yale have all recently hired at the senior level from abroad. These come on the heel of hirings from abroad pursuant to the drop in student enrollment in the late 1970s. Apparently, American Germanistik has failed to produce competitive candidates over the past two decades to qualify for some of the most prestigious positions.

Moreover, word has gotten around that American universities are more likely to hire foreign nationals who take their degrees from American institutions than they are to hire directly from European universities as was the case in the 60s and early 70s. Prompted by a bleak outlook at home and lured by the same pioneering spirit which enticed our forbearers, Germans, Austrians, and Swiss (also Czechs, Hungarians, and Rumanians who had the good fortune of learning German as a second language) enter our German programs in search of advanced degrees. They come also in the hope of pursuing a career at an American university (Goetschel 1993: 332). To be sure, we need

tendency to "enrich" German departments from without with new emigrants, Goetschel displays no ironic stance and reveals no sense of conflict with his opening statement that "exercises in the self-representation of one's own discipline omit regularly and not incidentally precisely that dimension which should be in the forefront of such critical reflection: the problematic preconditions of such self-representation itself. That might explain the singular, almost pungent self-referentiality of the self-portraits of *Germanistik*." The problematic preconditions of such self-portraiture might possibly include the portrait artist her or himself. It is worthy to note in this regard that three of the four most recent self-representations of our profession were occasioned and edited by Germanists attracted to the American academy from abroad (Lützeler, Trommler, Goetschel). Only the American one (Van Cleve/Willson) is vitriolic and untempered. One cannot help but wonder whatever happened to the frequently formulated insight—here I quote Victor Lange—that "the seemingly self-evident magisterial or preceptorial role of German *Germanistik* has (in the context of American presuppositions) possibly been harmful rather than productive"? Cf. Victor Lange, "The History of German Studies in America: Ends and Means," in *Teaching German in America* (1988), 13 (first published in *Monatshefte* 57 [1983]: 245-56).

new blood from abroad. No question about it. It is in the nature of our profession. However, is it in the nature of our profession to remain / to be "eine Einwandererwissenschaft"? The whole issue is becoming ever murkier as applications from the People's Republic of China to graduate programs in German are on the rise.

The historians seemed to have avoided this particular problem. But then they do not require native or near-native speakers as cheap classroom labor. Nor do they have to contend with an informal expectation that they write at least occasionally in German to impress the colleagues who pass tenure and promotion judgments. By publishing in German we also have a better chance of getting noticed by colleagues in Germany. Historians do not have that problem (at least, not to the same degree). Then, of course, German historians are not housed separately from other historians, while Germanists are indeed housed separately from other literary historians and critics.

The second aspect of the problem has to do not only with differing cultural conceptions (German, American), but also with differing views of how another culture is to be assessed. A handy catchword for getting at the heart of the matter is the cliché of the American pioneer spirit. Frank Trommler argues that what distinguishes the American mentality from the German/European mentality is that Europeans see themselves as acquiring legitimation through their integration in the whole of society and from being part of a long inward-looking tradition.[17] Americans, on the other hand, draw their sense of self and legitimacy from life on the frontiers: whether on the frontiers of the West, of science, of cutting-edge technology, marketing techniques, or whatever: "Das amerikanische Kulturkonzept lebt von der Grenze (frontier), nicht von der Totalität."[18] The action is at the edge, not at the center. The self is formed through the dialectic of interaction

at the margins, not quietly (and perhaps uncritically?) imbibed in the womb of the larger community. Hohendahl also privileges the

---

[17] The systems-theory paradigm advanced since the late 1960s by such thinkers as Nikolas Luhmann, Jürgen Habermas, S. J. Schmidt and others are, I think, expressions of this general phenomenon.

[18] Frank Trommler, "Über die Lesbarkeit der deutschen Literatur," in *Germanistik in den USA*, 224; see also 236.

boundary area, since shifting boundaries define the enclosed area and thus redefine the discipline. True, it is more difficult to envision what the new boundaries of an interdisciplinary Germanics would look like (Hohendahl, 1989: 233), but our task should be to stake out the territory and carve out the roads. We have already felled the trees.

If the theses of "Germanistik als Einwandererwissenschaft" and of American cultural production as "Polaritätsdenken in immer neuen Ausformungen" (Trommler 1989: 237) are accurate, the endless debate on the role of Germanistik in the USA may itself be the perfect expression of those determining factors which shape our professional identification in no-man's land. In that case, there would be little hope of concrete action resulting from this symposium. We would merely confirm what Thomas Steinfeld recently concluded about the verbiage produced by the meeting of German Germanists in Aachen: "Was immer die Germanisten tun: keiner erwartet von ihnen einen trefflichen Rat für den nächsten Tag" (FAZ 1994: N5). However, the early pioneers—and the later ones too -carved out of the wilderness a new home for themselves. If it was possible to do that in the wilds of Wisconsin and the board rooms of international conglomerates, it should be possible in the hallowed halls of academia.

Maybe we American Germanists can solve our problems more readily than our colleagues in Germany because we can draw upon American know-how. Our American know-how teaches us how to define a task in precise fashion so that we can solve it in a practical manner. Previous attempts to define the problem have paid too little attention, I think, to the pervasive double optics which impact upon our educational goals, our hiring preferences, our editorial decisions, and our tenure recommendations. We cannot hope to solve the problem until we have succeeded in defining it completely. We definitely need to define Germanics in the USA from outside the discipline as well as from within it.[19]

[19] Goetschel notes quite rightly: "Insofern Identität stets den Ausdruck einer Krise signalisiert, muß denn Germanistik so lange fragwürdig bleiben, wie sie sich auf ihrem eigenen Grund einzurichten sucht. Denn dieser Grund besteht aus Sedimentationen, gebildet aus ideologischen Kompensationen" (1993: 333).

But we would do well to avoid the vagueness inherent in such circumlocutions as, for example, when Jeff Peck avers: "German Studies, as a discursive formation becomes that site or strategic location where the discipline reflects upon itself and its practices, both critical and academic, where the variety of discourses about Germany—the literary, political, sociological—converge or diverge."[20] More recently, Heidrun Suhr recently remarked that "there is no definition of German Studies and there is no German-Studies theory" (Suhr 1992: 118). No wonder then that there is so much imprecision in the discourse on the nature of German Studies. In order not to muddy the waters further, I have sought to avoid the term, German Studies," as much as possible. We need, I think, to define what we do as precisely and consciously as we can, for the way we define what we do affects what we do ... and how we are perceived by others.

The very fact that this Vanderbilt conference is taking place at all is surely a cause of consternation to at least some in this room. Given the plethora of books, articles, and conferences on the topic of rethinking Germanistik and/or of plotting the future of German Studies in the United States, this conference should not even be necessary. The topic is old hat. There has been no lack of introspective inquiry and hopeful recommendations for change. The theoretical and practical ground has been well covered. Yet a broad sense of "Fachmisere," of persistent indecision in German departments and the split identities of many American Germanists is a tell-tale sign that the problem has not been fixed. In some quarters the suspicion is arising that the problem plaguing Germanistik in the USA is not fixable. Yet your ready, even enthusiastic, acceptance of an invitation to participate in this symposium is an indication that belief in the possibility of change is well and alive. Such change, however, will not come easily. We do well to recall Trommler's word of caution: "In einer so eingesessenen Disziplin kann es darum keine Überwindung der Isolation ohne Abbau an gewohnter Identität geben.... Eine

---

[20] Jeffrey Peck, "There's No Place Like Home? Remapping the Topography of German Studies," in *The German Quarterly* 62.2 (1989): 178-89, here 184.

qualitativ andere Disposition der Departments wird notwendig, für die die geistigen und personellen Voraussetzungen erst langsam zustandekommen" ("Einleitung," 1989: 15).

The fact that we are meeting here in Nashville, the mecca of that great American cultural phenomenon, country music, is perhaps already a sign of change. No, this is not Madison, Berkeley, or Philadelphia. It is a stronghold of American culture and represents a kind of new frontier. Maybe we do work best at the margins. But in no case should we unquestionably assume that by exchanging the center for the periphery we would thereby automatically eliminate the no-man's land of Germanics in the American academic landscape.[21] Let it not be said of us that we engaged in two-and one-half days of debate but could not come up with any sound and pragmatic advice on how to fix things.

[21] Cf. Sibley Fries 1993: "Verbinden wir das Eigenartige der Frau mit dem Eigenartigen ihrer gesellschaftlichen und geschichtlichen Umstände—und dies anhand der methodologischen Ansätze der Anthropologie, der Kulturgeschichte, des Feminismus, der Soziologie—, dann wird es vielleicht möglich sein, Deutsch im größeren Rahmen zu stabilisieren, das Verhältnis zwischen Zentrum und Peripherie auf den Kopf zu stellen und das "Niemandsland" der Germanistik in der akademischen Landschaft Amerikas aufzuheben" (421).

2

Reform or Retreat: Whither American Germanics? The Language of Reform

JOHN VAN CLEVE
Mississippi State University

I am pleased to be here—more precisely, I am relieved to be here, because for several years I have entertained the possibility that any remarks on the needed reform of German Studies in the United States might fall on deaf ears. But it no longer seems possible that the advisability of change will *not* be debated. Still possible, however, is the following familiar scenario: we meet, speak, and shake our heads. Then publish the head shaking. Then elect a task force or two. Then ... then many of us weary of the crisis in our field just as the latest hermeneutic school from France or the latest pedagogical method from the coast (your choice of coasts) begins to blossom into special sessions at the MLA Convention.

Surely this is one well-trod avenue of retreat: after all, our profession has been on it before. Two decades ago, as soon as it had become apparent that a significant loss in German enrollment was underway, an emergency meeting was held at the MLA Convention. That was December 1973. In the fall of 1975, a conference of leaders took place at the University of Wisconsin; the twenty-eight papers presented there proposed innovations in courses, curricula, and programs. The papers were published, and soon *Monatshefte* was devoting much of the space in each fall issue to articles concerning such new approaches and to the adoption of innovations across the country. The response to the crisis had been institutionalized in an understandably reactive and structurally traditional form. I say "understandably" because at the time there was no recent precedent for crisis management. So in the absence of such precedent, our colleagues responded as academicians usually respond: with serial publications and with new course proposals.

We would be beating a retreat, if we were to head down that avenue now. It did not take our colleagues of 1973 to their destination—higher enrollments. It failed. Between 1968 and 1986 we lost a staggering 44% of our undergraduate enrollment. The response so traditional in higher education, publications and courses, failed. To recognize the existence of a continuing crisis now, only to respond as they responded in 1973, would be to have learned nothing from history.

Analysis of our present situation suggests that we should use both the scientific method with which we are so comfortable and the common sense with which our deans are so comfortable. Having coauthored the tract that you have now endured, I still believe that there is great merit in this simple approach to a national reform.

It also has become clear to me that that tract rests on at least one tacit and ill-founded assumption—that we can use language as we have always used language. An analogy may be useful here. The feminism of the late 1960s and early 1970s first offered analyses of the most blatant and grievous examples of economic and social discrimination grounded in sexism. But soon it became apparent that the early analyses often suffered because of language bias. Feminism then had to begin work on what has amounted to a lexical reform movement.

Our profession has its own, much smaller language problem. After all, there are so few of us, and we are all sensitive to the value of precise speech. The problem affects us on campus with students, with colleagues, and with deans. It stands to affect our discussions here at Vanderbilt, for it touched the conference before this first session began.

Before I point out the problem, it behooves this guest to thank his hosts. The profession owes a debt of gratitude to John McCarthy, Richard Zipser, and the German Academic Exchange Service for gathering us all to confront matters many of which are troubling, even disagreeable. It took courage to call the conference. It took hard work to put it together. Thank you.

My conscience somewhat clearer, I shall play the discourteous guest by pointing out that the language problem to which I have alluded is to be found in the very title of the conference. The problem is the first word. Now, we have all studied language; we have all studied stylistics. Studied and taught. We are all familiar with the rule of thumb that the use of foreign words is to be avoided wherever possible—especially if an adequate native equivalent exists. The conference title violates that rule of thumb.

Some might respond by saying what others have said in the past: "There is no adequate English equivalent for the word *Germanistik*." One appropriate response to that sentiment is the following citation:

> germanics ... *n pl but sing in constr, usu cap:* the study of Germanic languages: Germanic philology.

The same source offers the following definition for the word "philology":

> the study of literature that includes or may include grammar, criticism, literary history, language history, systems of writing and anything else that is relevant to literature or to language as used in literature.

By extension then, my source, *Webster's Third New International Dictionary*, understands "Germanics" to be the study of Germanic languages or the study of Germanic literatures that includes or may include grammar, criticism, literary history, language history, systems of writing and anything else that is relevant to Germanic literatures or to Germanic languages as used in Germanic literatures. Now perhaps some nuances of meaning are missing here, but it seems to me that the word so understood is an adequate English equivalent for the word *Germanistik*. By the way, the same source cites the word "germanistics ... n pl but sing in constr, usu cap" only to refer in small caps to the word "germanics."

Some might respond by saying that it is not easy to use the word "germanics" because it is a neologism. Of course, some if not most of those who would make that argument have used the word "deconstruction," a neologism that does not appear in the unabridged Webster's I have cited here. My Webster's was printed in 1967.

Some questions are in order: What is our field? Can we finally agree to use the English word sufficiently familiar a quarter of a century ago to be defined, adequately defined by Merriam-Webster? What are we? *Germanisten* and *Germanistinnen*? Or can we finally agree to use the English word for which the *Oxford English Dictionary* cites a first written usage by Thomas Carlyle, *the* Carlyle, in 1831? The earliest citation offered by the *Deutsches Wörterbuch* for the word "Germanist" is from 1846. As we use the words, the English noun has a slightly longer pedigree than the German.

If we do not use the two adequate English words "Germanics" and "Germanist," no one will. If we do not conceive of what we do as an integral part of the mission of the *American* academy, no one will. When we are not in the German classrooms of that academy, we should think in the language of that academy: English. We should conceive of ourselves as American *Germanists*, of our field as American *Germanics* if we are to present ourselves as such to students, to faculty colleagues, and of course to those deans. They do not immediately understand the word *Germanistik*. So, if it is the only word in use, they will not understand what we do. Unless we are there every time we are discussed—every time two undergraduate students talk courses at a bike rack, every time the dean and the associate dean talk staffing at a water cooler. It is high time we began to offer other members of the American academy understandable answers to the questions "Who are you?", "What do you do?", and "How does that contribute to an *American* liberal arts education?"

To use German words to describe who we are and what we do is to use the German language to maintain a wall between us and the rest of the American academy. I consider it perverse to use the very language whose study we try to promote as a wall that prevents contact with students, campus colleagues, and administrators.

I have a gifted colleague who works in the English Department at Mississippi State University. He writes novels and conducts research on English Romanticism. Now and then he has asked me questions about German Romanticism. Pat does not know any German. I have often imagined my colleague trolling the current periodicals room, glancing at the covers of the learned journals that lie on those long oak tables that every university library seems to have. The cover of *The German Quarterly* catches his eye; he picks up the issue; he pages through. And American Germanics has made contact with a colleague in a related field. But what if the cover of *Monatshefte* catches his eye. "Mo-nat-sheeft." No contact. What about other colleagues, colleagues who study TESOL or language pedagogy? They go to the current periodicals room, too. "Die Unter-ikt-sprax ..." No contact. Surely the title *Teaching German* would be an adequate equivalent for *Die Unterrichtspraxis*. My colleague Pat will not pick up *Monatshefte*, but he would pick up *The Journal of American Germanics*. Our journal titles, our journal articles, and our conference talks should be in English. And we should use the words "Germanist" and "Germanics" at every opportunity.

Our use of the German language in inappropriate professional contexts is still hindering access by our American students and our American colleagues to the culture of German-speaking Europe. When on campus, we should speak as the dean speaks. If we are willing to be practical. The American Germanist who is not even willing to call himself or herself a Germanist will probably oppose the idea of an agenda for American Germanics. Such a colleague will not accept the proposition that the missions of German Germanics and American Germanics are profoundly different.

If the rest of us can, then we can move on to the proposition that the on-going crisis calls for an organized, national response. I note with enthusiasm the idea of an "Action Agenda for the Twenty-first Century" as the title of the Sunday morning discussion here. That final, so-appropriate title could not provide a more timely topic for a gathering of American Germanists in 1994.

3

The American-German Divide

PETER UWE HOHENDAHL
Cornell University

When I accepted the invitation to address the problem of German-American relations in our profession, that is, the relationship between American-born and European-born colleagues, I did not realize immediately that I took on a task that might very well get me into trouble. The topic is definitely emotionally charged on both sides of the divide, but specifically on the American side. Although we join the same professional organizations, for instance the AATG or the GSA, not to mention the MLA, and although our colleagues in other literatures refer to us as the Germans (with absolutely no regard for place of birth or citizenship), we feel very deeply about the divide between Americans and Germans. The differences are rarely addressed in official professional statements, but they are very much on the minds of those who attend departmental meetings, workshops and conferences. They play a role, frequently not acknowledged, in the process of hiring faculty, and they have an impact on the admission of graduate students. For the most part, however, these differences reveal themselves in private conversations, outside the public sphere where statements have to be legitimized in terms of rational professional arguments. When one listens to the rhetoric of these private conversations, it becomes quite clear that more is at stake than different positions on pedagogy and the literary canon. Such differ-

ences of opinion, in unacknowledged cultural assumptions and predispositions, tend to resist analysis. I hesitate to call them irrational
because by doing so I would merely invoke a well-known and not
necessarily fruitful dichotomy between irrational impulses on the
one hand and rational arguments on the other. And I suspect that this
approach to my question would possibly result in more confusion
and resentment.

Resentment, however, is definitely involved on both sides. It
manifests itself in descriptions of the other side that tend to border
on caricatures. In the American discourse there is a stereotype of the
German scholar that draws heavily on the Mark Twain tradition and
its insistence on the cumbersome Teutonic character of the German
language. The German discourse on the other hand relies on a notion
of high culture that tends to marginalize the American Germanist
(student or faculty member). An American graduate student at Ohio
State once told me that she and her American fellow students in
Berlin at one point were so fed up with their German "Kommilito-
nen" that they were ready to make T-shirts for themselves bearing
the inscription "Wir sind so oberflächlich." Of course, this mocking
cultural gesture would only have increased the German suspicion because it has a specifically American touch. American assessments of
their German-born colleagues are not necessarily more gracious.
What I have found in the professional literature on German Studies
in the United States would suggest that German-born teachers and
scholars are out of touch, they know very little about this country
and its culture. Instead, they have narrow professional interests and
otherwise overrate the importance of their field in the United States.
It is not difficult to detect in these descriptions the stereotype of the
ignorant and fumbling immigrant, the know-nothing who should be
excluded from important decisions.

While the German discourse operates with an opposition of
"Wissenschaft" and "Dilettantismus," in which the positive category
is then reserved for Germans, the American discourse operates with
the distinction between a native (English-American) culture and foreign cultures in which the foreign becomes the Other, i.e., the possibly interesting, but ultimately suspicious and problematic side. A
small anecdote might illustrate this point. Some time ago a member

of the English Department at Cornell suggested to me that she could not really recommend an Italian-born visiting professor to her students, since a native of Italy could not be intimately familiar with Shakespeare. In her mind this position was clearly reserved for Anglo-American scholars. I did not have the courage to tell her that many years before, when I was still a graduate student in Germany, an English professor of English literature informed me that only Englishmen but not Americans could speak with authority about Shakespeare. Neither of these intelligent and well-informed colleagues was aware of the assumptions which operated in their discourse. Similar things must be said about the German-American divide. It is grounded in unacknowledged cultural presuppositions. They have resulted in limiting and debilitating stereotypes that hinder our work.

I want to address this problem in the form of six theses. The first one looks at the nature of cultural knowledge and the consequences for approaching foreign cultures, in our case German culture and literature. My second thesis focuses more specifically on the question of "Auslandsgermanistik," that is to say, the perspective of our colleagues in Germany when they deal with German Studies in other countries. My third thesis addresses the problem of localism or nativism, i.e., the insistence on the predominance of the native culture over the foreign culture as an object of study. The fourth thesis turns to the use of cultural difference. What specifically could be the task of German Studies in the United States? My fifth thesis focuses on the question of language, more specifically on the relationship between the teaching of language and the teaching of culture. And last, but not least, I want to address the multicultural problematic and what it means for German Studies in this country.

1. The acquisition and dissemination of cultural knowledge appears to have its own rules. At least, I cannot imagine that in the field of chemistry an American professor would argue that French scholars are fundamentally incapable of understanding and appreciating certain aspects of chemistry. When my colleague at Cornell insisted on the special character of literary scholarship, a character that emerges from a native familiarity with the language of the literary text she emphasized qualities that supposedly cannot be learned. This kind of understanding is seemingly unmediated and based on in-

trospection. In this reading only a shared cultural environment enables the interpreter and teacher to open the text for the student.

Moreover, cultural knowledge is particular knowledge. It resists the grasp of universal statements. In other words, cultural knowledge, for example the understanding of literature and cultural phenomena, is ultimately grounded in our lifeworld as opposed to the sphere of the social system. Of course, once we institutionalize this knowledge in the form of professional organizations we have redefined it in the sphere of the cultural subsystem. Yet the grounding of cultural knowledge in the lifeworld is indispensable for the process of professionalization and the creation of expert knowledge. By relying on the lifeworld in which we grow up we also privilege our own culture and its practices over other cultures, which are seen as outside of comfortable boundaries. As a result, we tend to deny members of other cultures complete understanding of and full participation in our own culture. By understanding I mean an intuitive and unreflected grasp of and sharing in the cultural practices which surround us, which then can be extended to more articulated theoretical and historical forms of interpretation. This intuitive grasp, however, becomes important for the definition of our personal as well as collective identity. Sharing cultural objects, such as a writer or works of literature, within a community, even if we as its members disagree about their value and significance for ourselves and the community, defines our relationship to those whom we consider as standing outside the boundaries.

When we look at the American-German divide in our profession, these rules of inclusion and exclusion work both ways. For the German-born Germanist, whether he or she teaches in Germany or in the United States, the familiarity with German culture and literature is taken for granted, it is seen as a property that is shared within the German cultural community. (For brevity's sake, I disregard the differences between German, Swiss, and Austrian participants). As far as the academic role is concerned, the task then appears to consist of disseminating the body of knowledge available within the community. While the American student of German culture participates in the task of disseminating cultural knowledge the question of access is different, since the American scholar has to cross a cultural bound-

ary and cannot start out with the same degree of intuitive understanding. The American Germanist, on the other hand, places the
emphasis on the moment of reception and integration. The knowledge about German culture has to be made accessible to American
students. Now, from the viewpoint of reception, it is the German
scholar who is initially excluded since he or she does not share in an
intuitive understanding of American culture. In short, the German
emphasis on the origins of German culture stands against the American stress on the cultural environment into which the knowledge has
to be transferred.

2. My second thesis concerns the problematic in the term "Auslandsgermanistik," frequently employed in Germany for all students
of German literature and culture who either teach or study outside of
Germany. The seemingly neutral term is based on the model I developed in my first thesis, namely that cultural knowledge is grounded
in particular communities and therefore contains both the moment
of inclusion and of exclusion according to the position of the subject
seeking access. The term "Auslandsgermanistik" implies a dichotomy between "Inland" and "Ausland," marking not only a
boundary but also a dominant position for the "Inland." In this
model Germanistik is conceived as a discipline that originates in
Germany as the institutionalized study of the German literary and
cultural tradition. In this version Germanistik is defined as a scholarly self-representation of the linguistic and cultural heritage from its
beginnings to the present.

By comparison "Auslandsgermanistik" is perceived as institutionally derivative; it refers to branch offices that have been opened
in foreign countries to disseminate the results of research and cultural theory. Obviously, this model, which is still accepted by many
of our colleagues in Germany, is blind to the problem of cultural
transfer and reception in another culture. It assumes that American
students, by learning German, turn into at least secondary participants, more or less eager to imitate existing cultural practices. It focuses predominantly on the object of study and fails to reflect on the
cultural environment in which the process of transfer is taking place.
In addition, the paradigm of "Auslandsgermanistik" constructs a hierarchy of knowledge based on the geographical and cultural location

of the subject. Those who are "im Inland" know more and better than those "im Ausland," without raising the question whether there could be different kinds of insight. The fact that an observer does not share the cultural presuppositions could also be a chance for a critical understanding of the other culture. I shall come back to this question in my fourth thesis. But first I want to direct your attention to the other end of the spectrum, namely the problematic defense of American nativism.

3. The nativist argument has been presented by a number of our American colleagues. It comes in various forms, some of which stress the economic side and underscore the importance of preserving jobs in German departments for Americans against the "pernicious intrusion" of foreigners. This argument is clearly part of the ongoing debate over the protection of American jobs and the need for curtailment of immigration. It takes on an aggressive stance under the model outlined in the previous thesis. If there is a hierarchy of knowledge and expertise based on the cultural origin of the faculty member, then native Germans or Austrians clearly have an advantage over Americans. Consequently, they become a threat that has to be "dealt with." In the academic debate, however, the nativist position has been primarily defended in terms of visibility and effectiveness. In this argument the German-born Germanists in this country are primarily responsible for the invisibility of German Studies in the United States. Since they (at least the older generation) frequently write and publish in German, so the argument goes, they do not contribute to the American discussion.

This critique points to the failure of traditional German Germanistik to cross national cultural boundaries. As an almost completely self-contained institution it is not motivated to interact with other cultures. The weakness of the nativist position has to do with its predominantly reactive character: it bemoans the suspected hegemony of the German cultural tradition in our profession. In their attempt to counter the German threat, nativists foreground the aspect of reception and therefore underscore the importance of the American cultural environment in which American German departments function. In doing so they frequently posit American culture as an unquestioned standard for the study of German culture and literature in the same way traditional German Germanistik has posited German culture as the only viable standard. Carried to an extreme, an unacknowledged notion of American culture in this paradigm functions as a filter that allows only those elements of German culture to pass which are compatible with this idea. To put it differently, the nativist discourse is in danger of setting up a preconceived opposition between the "good," i.e., compatible part and the "bad," i.e., incompatible part, of the foreign culture. Thus the problem of American nativism is ultimately that it mirrors German nativism.

4. In my fourth thesis I want to draw some tentative conclusions based on my critique of "Auslandsgermanistik" and American nativism. Both positions, I would argue, have a moment of truth insofar as they respond to the peculiar nature of cultural knowledge and its dependence on the position of the observer and/or participant. Yet they fail to make a clear analytical distinction between the role of the participant and the role of the observer, a distinction which in my opinion is necessary in order to understand and make use of cultural difference. Traditional German Germanistik conflates the role of the observer with that of the participant and remains therefore blind to its own limits. By and large the institution does not appreciate the possibility that observers coming from different cultures could make significant contributions precisely because they are not participants. American nativism on the other hand is aware of its role as an observer of a foreign culture with respect to German literature, but it also conflates the role of the observer and the participant when it comes to its own cultural environment. There is a tendency then to celebrate the importance of the American native ground for the study of German. Both positions recognize cultural alterity as something that is located outside, but they cannot deal with internal cultural difference. The crucial point, however, would be to accept and make use of cultural difference. In order to do this we have to overcome a false opposition that has plagued German Studies in this country. The solution cannot be found in models that refuse to reflect on the implications of cultural difference.

First of all, we have to remind ourselves that we as teachers and scholars are always at the same time participants and observers. The role as participant is an inevitable precondition for that of the observer, yet in the American-German divide this relationship takes on different forms. While the American student of German literature, at least when she or he lives and works in this country, finds him- or herself predominantly in an observer role vis-à-vis German culture, but takes the participant role in his or her American cultural environment for granted, the German-born Germanist in the United States finds him- or herself in a slightly different position. While the attitude towards German culture is that of a (possibly former) participant, the relationship to the American environment contains both aspects, that of the outside observer and that of the participant.

Essentialist cultural models have no use for this split; they emphasize the inside perspective and therefore conflate the participant and the observer roles. Against this position I want to underscore the advantages of the split. The moment of alienation contained in the separation of observer and participant is a fruitful one. It ultimately enables us to gain a critical perspective towards the object of study, precisely because it is not taken for granted. By the same token it enables us to question our own cultural background—its peculiarities and its limitations. For this reason, strange as it may sound, it may be useful for German graduate students to come to the United States to study German literature under the guidance of American teachers. Of equal importance is the alienating impact of German culture on American-born students, namely as a subversive element that works against a comfortable affirmative cultural self-definition.

5. This brings me to my fifth thesis, which is concerned with the use of German as a foreign language. In most American German departments the teaching of the German language and the teaching of German culture are seen as intimately connected. Without the knowledge of the German language there can be, it is assumed, no serious understanding of German literature and culture. I do not mean to challenge this argument, but I want to suggest that its use in our curricula has been too narrow. Linguistic competence has been considered a prerequisite for the study of German literature, especially for its canonized works. For the most part the learning process has been perceived as a sequence of stages: the study of the language precedes the study of the literature. Among other things it has been this emphasis on the acquisition of German that has isolated German De-

partments in the American university, since it has designated the German Department as foreign territory, whether its faculty members are German-born or not. But as John van Cleve and Leslie Willson have pointed out, the first contact with a foreign literature in many cases comes through translation. The desire to read *The Tin Drum* in the original is motivated by the experience of reading it or another German text in translation.

Therefore the relationship between the foreign target language and the native language of the student should be renegotiated. The learning process is not a one-way street from English to German, from no knowledge of the foreign language to complete competence. Rather, in the American context, the use of English as a medium of self-understanding is as important as the use of German. Without the interface between the two languages cultural transfer is not possible. Cultural transfer depends on translation in the broader sense of the term, i.e., on the linguistic and cultural demarcation of the position of the text within the receiving culture. Hence the actual interface and interplay becomes a crucial step in the learning process. The foreign language, in our case, German, contains the very alterity that the student wants to grasp and then articulate through the medium of English, just as much as the seeming familiarity of the English translation is subverted through the intervention of the foreign (German) text. In other words, it is counterproductive to deny or suppress the fact that the majority of our students in this country approach German literature and culture as native speakers of English and as participants in American culture, a position which determines, to use the terminology of phenomenology, their initial horizon of expectation.

6. In my final thesis I want to modify the model I have introduced by adding another complicating factor. So far I have assumed that German and American culture are neatly divided. One is outside of the other. Yet this not really the case. When we look at the tradition of German Studies in this country, the Midwest and parts of the South, for instance Texas, play a very important role. Here we find universities with strong traditions in German Studies, among them Minnesota, Wisconsin, Ohio, Indiana, Missouri, and Texas, to mention just a few. These are also the regions where during the nineteenth century German immigrants settled. It has been my personal

experience that this background, although in most cases there is not much left of it in terms of the use of the German language, makes a difference for the well-being and success of a German Department. In the larger public sphere the study of German culture is accepted as the study of one's heritage. Yet this factor has remained almost unarticulated. Modern German departments pay no or very little attention to American-German culture as part of the American tradition.

The reasons are well-known. Historically, World War I marks a watershed. The outcome of the war with the American intervention on the side of the Entente, seriously undermined the existence of German-American culture in the United States. The extension of the war into the sphere of culture resulted in the ban of German at schools and the suppression of German culture in general. The German-American community fell silent. Also, during the twentieth century, the ties between the German-American community and academic German departments became weaker and more problematic. Yet, if we want to become serious about the multicultural experience in the United States, we will have to face this past, now so foreign to most of us. I do not mean to suggest that this will be an easy task consisting of celebrating past achievements. But we will have to come to terms with it and recognize its relevance for the position of German Studies in this country. In other words, we are not merely dealing with a German-American divide, rather, we are at the same time dealing with a German component within American culture, a component that has been neglected for a number of reasons, among them political pressure from the outside and professional pressure from the inside, i.e., fixation on German high culture and its literary canon.

I have tried to show that the existing divide between American-born and German-born Germanists in this country is grounded in a problematic opposition which has hindered rather than furthered German Studies in this country. Neither the German model of Germanistik based on the notion of a German origin of our profession nor the American response to this position, namely nativism, provides an adequate answer to our present and future task, since both models move cultural difference to the outside. In this respect they mirror each other.

4

Response to Hohendahl[1]

LYNNE TATLOCK
Washington University

Many thanks to Professor Hohendahl for his brave attempt to address publicly a painful subject. Although Hohendahl has at times framed his remarks as if the American-German divide alluded to the split between our colleagues who practice in Europe and those of us who practice in North America, I believe that it is fair to say that the main issue at hand is a perceived American-German divide that affects the American teaching and research context, specifically the alleged divide between European-born colleagues and American-born colleagues in American German programs.

I am in sympathy with some of Hohendahl's points. I agree, for example, that we should rethink the relationship between the foreign target language and the native language of the majority of our students, namely English, and its effect on learning, and I believe that he is correct to assert that it is counterproductive to suppress the fact

---

[1] The paper also responds in part to John Van Cleve and A. Leslie Willson. *Remarks on the Needed Reform of German Studies in the United States* (Columbia, S.C.: Camden House, 1993). I assumed that the authors' chapter "A Critique of the Field" (15-23) prompted the organizers of the Nashville conference to devote a session to the "German-American Divide," and that their critique represents what Hohendahl chose to call an "American nativist" point of view.

that most of our students in this country approach German literature and culture as native speakers of English and as participants in American culture. I also agree that American German programs need to include study of the German-American heritage, that is German-American heritage understood in a broad and critical sense; it should, by the way, also include the cultural history of German Jews in America, a rich field much neglected because of the vexed political history of the twentieth century. We also need to examine with our students the impact of German *ideas* on mainstream American culture, in American Transcendentalism, for example.

Hohendahl has pointed out that the subject of the so-called American-German divide tends to be addressed privately rather than publicly. Obviously there are good reasons for this, not the least of which is that responsible academics who have devoted their lives to transmitting foreign cultures ought to shy away from confessing publicly to resentment against natives of those very cultures. Similarly, European-born academics who have chosen to build lives and careers in the United States, whose own children may for all intents and purposes be Americans, ought to find public confession of private discontent with American-born colleagues distasteful. And while I admit to my own reluctance to speak publicly about such issues, and while I realize that complicating the issue can be a way of avoiding the issue, I nevertheless have to insist that we cannot and should not speak of a simple division between American-born and European-born colleagues.

To speak as if the profession were somehow neatly cloven according to place of birth—and by place of birth I assume that Hohendahl means the language and culture that practitioners would claim as their birthright—hardly does credit to the complexities of the biographies of the real practitioners and to their diverse senses of community, of personal and professional allegiance, senses that may well vary over the course of their professional careers. And not only age, but gender, generation, and geography mediate our professional lives in significant ways that blur cultural origin. While I, for example, am American born and while I may occasionally protest that I am not a German, I know that the study of German literature, language, and culture has inexorably determined who I am. After all, I have been at it far longer than not.

As one American colleague in French Studies once remarked to me, German has even written itself on my face. She pointed to the way I spread my mouth and talked a little through my teeth. "But, Maryann, it's the same for you," I said, "look at your mouth, your whole face pushes forward to register 'French' skepticism." At one time there was nothing I wanted more than to pass as a German; I still play this foolish game from time to time when I am in Germany. I dare say there are many more American-born colleagues who are far more German-identified than I as a result of having lived many years abroad or of having a German partner. Conversely, I have a German-born colleague who sports cowboy boots and Hawaii shirts, and who drives a gigantic car, and who speaks of "those Germans" as though he weren't one. I expect that down the line I will have changed again—perhaps I will change many times—, and so will my colleague. The changes will depend on our life circumstances. Does this mean that he and I will always find ourselves opposing one another? Quite the contrary. So far we have found ourselves worrying together about our enrollments, worrying about our student's progress, worrying about all those things necessary to the health of a German program.

While I hesitate to take the low road after Hohendahl has taken the high one, I believe that since this conference addresses the present American context, the hard facts of diminishing resources deserve more prominence in an examination of the so-called American-German divide than Hohendahl gives it. Such a division would seem far less important if we had plenty of students and plenty of money. Hohendahl proposes that stressing the economics of the problem belongs to what he calls the American nativist argument. But speaking of economics need not necessarily lead to primitive arguments about the "importance of preserving jobs in German departments for Americans against the pernicious intrusion of foreigners." Precisely the economics of the problem has given rise to our sense of urgency, and is thus why we are here today.

Surely the present constitution of many German Departments—i.e., aging and "over-tenured," as our administrators like to say, results from the geopolitical conditions of twenty to thirty years ago.

Among other things the expansion of American universities in the 1960s opened up important opportunities for some enterprising European men; these men, now in their late fifties and sixties currently form a significant group in some German Departments. The degree to which the members of this group adapted to their new environment, the ways in which they transmitted their birth culture, I would submit, varied, and will continue to vary depending on their life histories, the location of their institutions, the degree to which they were accepted by and acquired influence in these institutions. If some of the members of this group seem to some of us to be responsible for our present woes or at least seem to be doing little to help us solve the present problems, we might do well to look at adjacent departments—English departments, history departments—where we will undoubtedly discover that the same age group of men were and are variously, but similarly inactive or intractable, having been socialized into academia and given tenure at a time when expectations were radically different from what they are now. In short, country of origin may not be the key factor and we may want to reconsider our framing of the problems.

We are well aware that the job market has been tight for years in the United States, but obviously it is not yet as tight here as it is abroad. While admittedly some of the positions advertised at North American institutions of higher learning largely amount to language instruction, hardly what a European might imagine as appropriate to the professorial rank, the United States nevertheless provides access to an academic career that is not available elsewhere. If European universities are effectively closed to younger generations, why wouldn't the young, still hopeful, and still flexible seek employment abroad? Furthermore, why wouldn't a young European, having been subjected to seminars with over a hundred people in them, want to consider an education in the United States where one receives individual attention, a generous stipend, and the vague promise of some kind of employment further down the line? Were it not for the fact that there continue to be new job openings in the United States and that the situation in Europe is relatively hopeless, Europeans would not find the United States so appealing in the first place, and we would, I hope, not be having this discussion at all. If there were more jobs and if Europeans were present in fewer numbers they would no doubt more likely be regarded as a precious commodity, vital to the health of the profession in America.

If we can believe our administrations, universities have never been so strapped financially in recent history. Many department chairs must repeatedly justify the existence of their departments by enrollments and numbers of undergraduate majors and minors. Departments must therefore seek colleagues who are well-rounded, who, while continuing to produce scholarship of high quality, can attract undergraduates; access to university resources depends on it. Hohendahl is correct to point to our emphasis on the "importance of the moment of reception and integration" of foreign culture, but this emphasis should not be seen merely as compensation for American-born scholars' cultural lack but rather as vital to the health of German programs. As the last twenty-five years have made quite clear, American undergraduates will vote with their feet if the material is not made accessible to them.

As European-born PhDs trained in America have proven and will continue to prove, European-born scholars are perfectly capable of learning to teach American undergraduates, of addressing precisely the moment of reception and integration. In short a person's ability to teach undergraduates effectively does not depend upon country or culture of origin, rather on personal qualities, training, and experience. Obviously the specific needs of American institutions will shape German programs in America; those who succeed in the American system will not be the same colleagues who would succeed in the European system. And given the current demographics and the continued pressure of affirmative action, it appears that those who will succeed in America are more likely than ever before to be women, both European and American born. In fact European born women have already found that North America offers them opportunities presently unthinkable in Europe.

Let me cite a final uncomfortable fact. The rift between the European-born and the American-born that many of us may in fact bridge successfully in our daily lives is enforced by United States law. Like it or not, when hiring we are required by law adequately to "test the American labor market." It is becoming increasingly difficult to work with the U.S. Department of Labor. If we wish to acquire permanent residency status for a new hire who is not a US citizen, we are now required not simply to argue that the candidate whom we have selected is the best in the pool but rather to argue that all other candidates were in some way inadequate, i.e., we have to specify why we did not hire each of the persons who applied. When the applications for a single job often number well over 150, it cannot help but give department chairs pause as they petition the Department of Labor on behalf of so-called aliens. What would it say about the ability of our graduate and undergraduate programs to serve American students if we were regularly to hire European-born candidates over American ones, claiming that all of the American-born candidates were inadequate? What does it say about our promises of future jobs to our hopeful European graduate students when their visa status (by law!) prejudices potential employers against them?

Hohendahl has offered some useful theses for thinking productively about the ways in which cultural origins position practitioners in our field. Nevertheless, while I understand what he means to say when he concludes that the German model of *Germanistik* and the American response to it in some respects mirror one another I think that such a tidy symmetry can obscure the practical exigencies of our current situation. I have tried to suggest (1) that practitioners do not necessarily feel a simple insider/outsider dichotomy that remains constant over time, (2) that there are additional divisions in the field that practitioners may at times feel more acutely than cultural divisions, e.g., gender, generation, geographical location of institution, and (3) that the geopolitical situation and current financial crises upset the symmetry that Hohendahl's concluding statement posits. Finally, with regard to current hiring practices, I have recalled that the division between American-born and European-born, which I personally would like to ignore, is currently enforced by law.

5

Graduate Education in German:
Past Experiences and Future Perspectives

ROBERT C. HOLUB
UC Berkeley

The program for this conference allots me fifteen minutes for my presentation today. Although I have a great deal to say about the topic of graduate education, I can sum up my talk in three points: (1) For the past two and a half decades we have been producing too many PhDs. (2) The overproduction of PhDs is a serious ethical, as well as a social problem, since the chief benefactors of this overproduction are the professors who are involved in graduate education. (3) We should make every effort to bring the number of PhDs in line with the number of new positions available, by (a) eliminating, combining, and reducing graduate programs, and (b) curtailing the hiring of foreign-trained scholars and the training for foreign students.

Let me comment briefly on each of these three points:

I. With regard to the current overproduction of PhDs, there will probably be very little dispute. When I first ventured onto the job market in 1979, a good, tenure-track job with an open specialization would attract about 100 applicants, a figure that meant many qualified PhDs would receive either no position or a position for which they were overqualified. Two years ago the German Department at Berkeley received approximately 100 applications for a one-year lecturer position which required a specialization in transition courses from lower-division instruction to the major; last year we received 83 applications for a one-year lecturer position specializing in lower-division language instruction and supervision. Doctoral students from our department who applied for positions at other universities reported as many as 500 applications for a single job. Although only one person will receive such a position, this does not mean that 499 will be unemployed. Some of the applicants no doubt already hold positions at other institutions and are pursuing a better professional opportunity, and some will be successful with one or another of their applications for jobs in higher education. But many of the 499, most of whom we must assume are qualified, competent teachers and potential scholars, will be unemployed, underemployed, or employed outside the profession for the upcoming academic year.

Perhaps those who are unsuccessful are in some ways more fortunate than those who manage to find employment at the margins of the profession, since the unsuccessful ones are more likely to direct their energies toward some other type of career. Those who find temporary employment frequently become part of the growing number of itinerant academic migrant workers, procuring a series of temporary positions; but only the most fortunate of these will secure, at some point in the future, a regular position that matches their qualifications. Still others from the 499 will land a tenure-track position, but for one reason or another will leave or be dismissed from their position and thus be left without any security; many of these people will again join the ranks of the unfortunate 499, sending in applications where the chances of success are becoming about as likely as winning the lottery.

Unfortunately, new and recent PhDs currently face a relatively unchanged situation over the past two decades despite the hills and valleys in hiring.[1] But statistics, such as those published periodically

---

[1] There was obviously a steep decline in the number of PhDs produced for a number of years, although not for every year, from the mid-seventies to the mid-eighties; the number has been on the rise for most fields since 1987. Significant in all the statistical studies I have consulted is that in spite of the rather precipitous decrease in the number of PhDs from 1976 until 1986 the prospects for a tenure-track job remained about the same. The reason for this must have been that the number of tenure-track jobs decreased just as rapidly.

by the MLA, indicate that over a fifteen year period starting in 1976-77 and extending through 1991-92 there was no year in which over 50% of new PhDs in foreign languages received tenure-track appointments.[2] I should also note that the statistics collected by the MLA are subject to inaccuracies in several areas. In the first place, the MLA relies upon the reports of departments on their own PhDs, and I consider it likely that a departmental report of its placement record is somewhat rosier than the reality.[3] Departments are also much more likely to have information on placements in tenure-track positions than in other types of positions, or on unemployed and underemployed PhDs, or those employed outside of the profession. Finally, in many years in which the MLA surveyed there was a significant number of people for whom the employment status was unknown. In 1986-87 this was the case for 17.6% of the new PhDs in the foreign languages; in 1991-92, for 7.9%. It is much more probable that PhDs with unknown employment status were underemployed or unemployed than that they held tenure-track positions. Thus even the official statistics are apt to be somewhat inflated when compared with what is really occurring. I would only note here that among the foreign languages German does rather poorly in terms of employment. But even in the most favorable field in the foreign languages—Spanish—the MLA documents that over one-third of new PhDs do not receive tenure-track positions.

[2] I am using here the information reported in Huber 1994. There are no data given for the years before 1976-77. In the report to the Executive Council, Huber et al. indicate that in 1991-92 51.1% of the English PhDs received tenure-track positions. Considering that departments reported an unknown employment status for 11.2% of English PhDs (121 PhDs out of the total of 1082 for the year), the actual figure is apt to be somewhat lower than 50% for English PhDs as well. That is, the MLA can confirm tenure-track positions for only 45.4% of PhDs from 1991-92 in English.

[3] At Berkeley I read last year about a survey done by our Graduate Division that "showed" how successful Berkeley departments have been in placing PhDs. The placement rate for new PhDs was cited at something close to 90%. The only trouble was that the Graduate Division depended solely on the reports of the individual departments. In the information supplied by departments, I know for a fact that there was a significant number of non-reports of employment status (which the Graduate Division, in turn, like the MLA, did not count in its final statistics).

Because of the inaccuracy of MLA statistics I have attempted to compile a statistic that is more meaningful. Taking the actual names of PhDs from the *Monatshefte*, i.e., those graduate students who received degrees in 1986-87, I looked up each name in the *Monatshefte Directory* (published in 1991 and purporting to represent the state of German Studies in 1990) to see how many of them had obtained a job by that time. From 79 PhDs granted in 1986-87 only 28 names appeared with assistant or associate professor positions in the *Directory*. I could find only 3 other people listed at all, all of whom had obviously not obtained a tenured position or a tenure-track position. The results of my findings are that only 35.4% of those who received PhDs in 1986-87 had obtained fairly secure academic employment by 1990 at normal four-year colleges or universities. Of course, the *Monatshefte Directory* does not contain information about every college and university in the country. It is highly probable that some of the remaining 60% (for whom I could find no information) had some kind of academic position somewhere. At many of the institutions that do not report to *Monatshefte*, however, it is likely that these PhDs will be underemployed, since the *Directory* contains entries from 481 institutions in the United States and Canada, certainly almost all of the institutions that grant any sort of degree in German. It is therefore unlikely that more than 50% of the PhDs from 1986-87 will ever obtain a job that matches their training in graduate school.

The employment situation may have been dismal in the past, and it may be dismal in the present, but what about the prospects for the future? Among the studies that deal with this thorny issue the best known is William Bowen and Julie Sosa's *Prospects for Faculty in the Arts and Sciences: A Study of Factors Affecting Demand and Supply, 1987-2012* (Princeton: Princeton UP, 1989). Since its appearance in 1989, Graduate Deans and educational optimists have relied on Bowen and Sosa, which I fondly abbreviate BS, to justify the continued training of graduate students. In this volume the authors predicted that the Golden Age of faculty employment did not lie behind us in the 1960s, but ahead of us in the 1990s. Theirs was a welcome message to a system of higher education that, in fields such as ours, had experienced a glut of PhDs for two decades, and perhaps the positive message accounts for the uncritical way in which their study was received in academia. In retrospect, of course, it is obvious that their account is fatally flawed and seriously dated in its predictions. Their analysis of demand, for example, makes unfounded assumptions concerning student/faculty ratios and student enrollment,[4] while their analysis of supply does not take into account the huge backlog of PhDs who have not found jobs or who, given increased demand, might climb back into the job market. Perhaps the most im-

---

[4] Their analysis of demand takes four scenarios that are apt to portray a rosier picture than has occurred and than will occur in our fields. The two variables that Bowen and Sosa use are student/faculty ratio and the arts-and-science's share of enrollment. They document that from 1977 until 1987 the student/faculty ratio decreased because proportionally fewer students enrolled in arts-and-science courses. (This is hardly a comforting fact for our field.) At the same time that fewer students were interested in our courses, the number of faculty increased from 119,863 in 1977 to 139,350 in 1987 (72). This combination of proportionally fewer students enrolled in arts-and-science courses and an increase in the number of arts-and-science faculty accounts for the decrease in the student/faculty ratio. One might be tempted to conclude that a reversal is bound to occur, and that the ratio would gradually rise over the next decade or so as faculty retire and as administrations recognize that the decline in enrollment and majors in certain fields does not warrant the same large number of faculty members. But Bowen and Sosa do not conclude this; in fact, they state that they "do not see a basis either in a priori reasoning or in historical evidence for anticipating general increases in student/faculty ratios" (83). One could counter that there is no reason to expect the ratio to continue to decrease or to remain constant either, and, indeed, Bowen and Sosa provide no further explanation for their odd assumption. In fact there is some evidence that the decline in arts-and-science enrollments may be rather permanent. David W. Breneman claims in *Liberal Arts Colleges: Thriving, Surviving, or Endangered?* that many colleges have survived the 1980s by switching the curriculum away from liberal arts to career training (see Magner). At the same time the prospects for hiring a larger number of faculty to educate this dwindling number of students seems rather poor given the fiscal realities of most colleges and universities. On the basis of their odd assumptions Bowen and Sosa include in their four model scenarios only one in which the ratio will again increase, and in this case (IV) they cancel the negative effect on the number of faculty positions by allowing the other variable, relative student enrollment in arts and sciences, to increase as well. The assumption of a relative increase in student enrollment is also not founded in argument.

If we check the real, empirical world, especially in our field, I believe that we have good reason to question the four optimistic scenarios presented by Bowen and Sosa. At Berkeley, for example, none of the four scenarios matches the actual course of events over the past few years. There has been a marked increase in the ratio of students/faculty without any noticeable increase in arts-and-science enrollment versus other fields. The result is that fewer faculty are doing more teaching in terms of numbers of students. Without any decline in students, the Berkeley campus now operates

portant factor missing from their study, however, is an analysis of the funding sources for colleges and universities. There may be a need for new faculty, but if there are no funds, there will be no hiring, and universities will find other, "creative" ways to cope with student needs. The presupposition that we will get up to the old numbers after funding is restored, presumes (a) that funding levels will indeed go up again, and (b) that new structures, methods, and teaching practices will not have been introduced that eliminate the need for new faculty. During the past two years funding has, in fact, gone down from many state capitals,[5] and there are indications from some

with over 200 fewer faculty members, and most of these cuts, we have been informed, are permanent cuts to the college and professional schools, not temporary cuts that will be restored at some later date. This is not a scenario that Bowen and Sosa entertain, but since it is reality, one would have to grant that it is just as likely as any scenario that they sketch in their volume.

I should mention that there are other problems with the uncritical use of student/faculty ratios. One of the ways in which faculty hiring can be affected has to do not only with how many students we teach in each course, but also with how many courses we teach. It is difficult to say what will occur, but again we should be cautious rather than giddy. Colleagues at other universities have told me that their institutions were seriously considering changing the standard teaching load for professors in the humanities by adding an extra course per year. One does not have to be an economist or statistician to figure out that an increase in teaching load will eliminate a large percentage of the potential new positions from retirement and from other forms of attrition. In short, the ratios that Bowen and Sosa use may or may not conform to what will occur, but I have no reason to believe that their view is any more sound than a view that would predict increased ratios or—what amounts to the same thing with regard to faculty positions-increased teaching load.

The other variable that Bowen and Sosa use is enrollment. They detect a declining share of enrollment in the arts and sciences from 31.2% in 1976-77 to 24.9% in 1984-85, but they assume—with some justification—that there will be a floor beneath which enrollments will not drop. It is rather alarming, however, that the drop in the humanities' share of enrollment has been so severe: from 17.4% to 13.1% over that same eight-year period, and that in 1987 the humanities had fewer than 5% of all majors. In any case, Bowen and Sosa provide no reason to make anyone believe that our share of enrollment (English and the foreign languages) will increase, and, as I have just pointed out, even if there should be an increase, there is no reason for anyone to believe that this increase will necessarily have a positive impact on the number of faculty positions.

[5] The *Chronicle of Higher Education* indicated that the 1993-94 appropriations from state governments for higher education had risen by 2% in absolute terms over a two-year period, but had dropped by 4% when adjusted for inflation. In 28 states appropriations were lower than two years ago when adjusted for inflation; four states had no change.

states, such as my own, that it is not likely to reach peak levels again. Many private universities appear to be suffering a fate similar to public institutions. Newspaper reports that a department or even a series of departments are being closed at major institutions are no longer surprising. Thus instead of the PhD shortages and employment opportunities that Bowen and Sosa prophesied, "downsizing" has become the watchword of the 1990s.

II. My second point—that the overproduction of PhDs is a serious ethical problem for professors at institutions in graduate training because they profit from the continuation of the system—is apt to be more hotly disputed. One of the reasons for this is that the notion of profit or benefit is difficult to measure. Some of my colleagues could very easily present the following argument: "Aren't the real beneficiaries of graduate education the graduate students? After all, we, as their mentors, sacrifice a good deal of time and effort in seminars with them. And after they finish these seminars, we put in long, hard hours supervising their dissertations. The more conscientious among us even spend time assisting them in finding a job, and afterwards, in furthering their careers. And isn't the other beneficiary of our efforts the institutions at which we teach, which gain prestige through our sacrifices for the graduate program? We certainly feel bad that many graduate students do not procure adequate employment; but this is not our responsibility; nor is it to our advantage." Let me answer these colleagues with the following counter-scenario.

Professors benefit by graduate programs in three ways. (I ignore here the psychological and psychosexual benefits that arise from the stroking of the professor's ego, and the exposure of male professors to a new crop of young, admiring women students, two factors which are not inconsiderable in the real, existing world of graduate education.) In the first place the presence of graduate students allows them to teach their own, often rather narrow, fields of study. It provides them, therefore, with a captive audience, and often with a group that is then compelled to adopt their interests and assist them with their research. Second, graduate education most often provides teachers for courses that professors do not want to teach, and graders for papers and examinations that they do not want to grade. Involvement in graduate education thus usually frees up more time than it occupies, and that time can be used to further the research careers of the faculty at graduate institutions. Finally, the very fact that an institution possesses a graduate program enhances the reputation of the professorate that teaches there. Not only do individual professors get to spread their fame by producing protégés around the country—if any of them manage to get jobs, that is—but they also appear to stand above colleagues at purely undergraduate schools, even when these institutions have a better undergraduate population. Indeed, the ferocity with which the faculty clings to graduate programs even though the field is demonstrably overpopulated should give us the best indication of whose interest is really being served by graduate education.

But if we professors in graduate education are benefiting from the continuation of a system of education in which 50% or more of our students do not obtain adequate employment, then why is it that so few of us feel morally responsible? Part of the answer to this is that we displace our responsibility onto the graduate students: although we benefit from their presence, we reason that they know the risks and should therefore assume the moral burden for their own actions in attending graduate school. In good capitalist fashion we shrug our shoulders and pronounce the magic phrase: *caveat emptor*. But for those of us who are less cynical another part of the answer is that we very rarely take note of the problem on more than an individual or departmental level. From the perspective of the department, we try to establish good programs and prepare students well for a career as college and university teachers. In our interactions with individual students, we do our best to provide adequate training and supervision. In short, we try to effect the things over which we have some control—but we ignore everything else. It would be absurd for any single graduate program to curtail its admissions voluntarily, because some other program would no doubt simply pick up the slack. Similarly it would do us as individuals no good to refuse participation in graduate training, because our colleagues would just shift their focus slightly to make up for our refusal. Thus we are able to avoid the ethical consequences of our own actions by restricting our purview to the local and the immediate level of our activity.

III. The third point I would like to make is that we should do everything we can to eradicate the overproduction of PhDs. While I believe we as a group and a profession should be in the forefront of demanding an expansion of employment opportunities, it would be foolish to think that the current imbalance can be eliminated solely through the creation of more jobs. The reality of funding is that there will simply not be enough demand for PhDs unless we reduce the supply. The main way that we can correct the imbalance is therefore to reduce graduate education. But it is not easy to accomplish such a reduction because there is no national organization that occupies itself with such matters. The MLA has often commented on the job market, offered seminars for job seekers, and provided statistics; but it has never suggested any means to solve the problem of excess PhDs except at the employment end of the process—when it is already too late for the young men and women who have spent time, money, and effort on a career that will never materialize. I believe we need to bring these issues more to the forefront in professional discussions, not just in German, and not just in English and foreign languages, but in the humanities and social sciences in general, and even across the spectrum of the university. Our professional organizations need to recognize that they have the moral responsibility to represent not just the named and distinguished professors at prestige institutions, but also the young men and women who hope to enter the profession.

In addition to pressuring professional organizations to adopt proactive policies, I would recommend that we consider the following two propositions: (1) We should oppose as a profession the hiring of foreign-trained scholars as long as we are overproducing PhDs. We are all aware of several recent appointments of such scholars (and many over the past two decades), and although I believe that in most cases the department in question obtained an excellent researcher, I am equally convinced that the faculty, the university, and the profession abrogated its responsibility to its own students by allowing such appointments to occur. When I have spoken to colleagues about this matter, I have often been told that these appointments are usually made at a senior level, and that they are justified because the department needed an established scholar. This is rationalized nonsense, first because there are many fine, established scholars at institutions across the country—and if there are not, we should really question the efficacy of our graduate programs—and second because simple arithmetic reveals that with x number of positions in the profession, the reduction of this number of positions by one will mean that somewhere, at some level, one of our students will not receive employment. The absurdity of the situation is that most often the employment of a foreign-trained scholar is justified as a necessary addition for advanced degree programs that will simply reinforce the cycle of the overproduction of PhDs.

(2) We should oppose graduate programs that exist by importing foreign students into the American classroom. Again we are all aware of several programs in German that either cannot attract American students or that prefer to train German students. In these programs, more than others, it is evident that graduate education is carried out not for the benefit of the university or the undergraduate students, but for the professorate. These foreign students often go on to compete—often rather successfully because of their linguistic competence—with American colleagues. Like most of you, I believe that foreign-trained scholars and foreign students enrich our programs. But it is just as obvious that there are other ways to include them in our institutions besides placing them in direct competition with our native students. If we are going to correct the imbalance of PhDs produced and hired, then the curtailment of foreign-trained hires and foreign students would be a good place to start our efforts.

The three points I have argued are meant as provocations for this conference and to the profession. German is only one of many fields in which these matters should be discussed—but probably will not be discussed. My pessimism in this regard stems from experience and observation: if we have not done anything to correct this situation in almost a quarter of a century, why should we do anything now, especially when, as I have argued, it is against our interest as professors to deal rationally and nationally with graduate education? If we have been able to assuage the pangs of our collective conscience for so many years, why would the 1990s or the advent of a new millennium suddenly arouse us from our professionally irresponsible slumber?

Works Cited

Bowen, William G., and Julie Ann Sosa. *Prospects for Faculty in the Arts and Sciences: A Study of Factors Affecting Demand and Supply, 1987-2012*. Princeton: Princeton UP, 1989.

Huber, Bettina J. et al. "Annex No. 8: Report on the Job Information Service" (ms. presented to the Executive Council Meeting 25-26 February 194).

Lively, Kit. "State Support for Public Colleges Up 2% This Year." *Chronicleof Higher Education* (27 October 1993): A29, A32-A34.

Magner, Denise K. "Many Colleges Have Survived by Moving Away From the Liberal Arts, Author of New Book Says." *Chronicle of Higher Education* (2 March 1994): A18.

Nollendorfs, Valters, and Geoffrey S. Koby. *Directory of German Studies: Departments, Programs, and Faculties in the United States and Canada 1990*. New York: German Studies Information Limited, 1991.

"Personalia 1987/88." *Monatshefte* 79.3 (1987): 320-66.

6

How Visible Are We Now?

HEIDI BYRNES
Georgetown University

The two previous sessions in this conference have defined the problem, set parameters for discussion, and have provided an overview of who we are as members of the profession of Germanistik in general.

I take it as the goal of this session, "Visibility in the Academy: Positionings" that we look at ourselves in terms of the institutional context within which we live, rather than in terms of a general, shared professional identity. I take that perspective to be not just another way for arriving at a more complete picture of *Germanistik* in the USA. Instead, I consider the increasing weight being given throughout American higher education to a variety of aspects of faculty life that are marked by an explicit and direct tie-in to the institution to amount to a redefinition of the professorate as compared with approximately the last fifty years. Not coincidentally, those roughly fifty years were the years of the cold war, a period in which massive federal and foundation support of all disciplines created an identity for faculty—some might say allowed faculty to ratchet up an identity for themselves—that differs dramatically from the one that had prevailed for most of the first half of the century, indeed for much of American higher education.

It would be folly to claim that we will or should return to that earlier state of faculty life, when faculty were almost exclusively defined by student and institution, sometimes at the expense of scholarship, but certainly without the perquisites of freely-moving entrepreneurialism and connections around the world. Nevertheless, it is abundantly clear that the end of the cold war has implications not only in international politics and defense but also for professors' lives in the academy. Gradually the preconditions for the dominant model are disappearing: among them rich outside funding, relatively well-off institutions, a supportive and even respectful public, and a favorable job market that does not have to consider seriously, much less learn to live with, emerging alternative modes and media for delivering education or accessing information and knowledge. With them vanishes the primacy, even desirability of the faculty star, fixed or wandering, whose first allegiance is to the discipline or, to put it crassly, to a very small group of colleagues with whom he or she discourses regularly at professional meetings that, for all intents and purposes, could take place anywhere around the globe. I realize, of course, that very few faculty members could and did live such lives. But that is not the point.

What is critical is that the reward system for faculty, no matter what the nature, location, mission, or identity of their home institutions, not to mention the students whom these institutions purported to serve, was constructed to uphold, perpetuate, even privilege that ideal over other ways in which faculty had previously thought of themselves, namely primarily as educators of students at a particular crucial moment of passage into responsible adulthood.

Instead, we are in the midst of a redefinition of scholarship that seems much closer to where most faculty members have traditionally lived their lives in any case. To give just one, by now well-known example, let me refer to the four categories for scholarship identified in Ernest Boyer's influential report "Scholarship Reconsidered: The Priorities of the Professoriate," where the scholarship of discovery, of application, of integration, and of teaching, all have strong institutional tie-ins. Their underlying ethos is derived from an orientation toward others, be they students, be they teams of other researchers, as in interdisciplinary ventures, or the adjacent community, or issues and problems in society at large as they can be addressed on the ground from the vantage point and with the capabilities of a given institution.

While Boyer can still be considered to speak from within the academy, there are powerful outside forces demanding that the professoriate rethink itself. The public is clamoring for a renewed emphasis on teaching, not primarily on original research, since, rightly or wrongly, it sees our teaching and not our scholarship as tied to the kind of learning that is required for our students' future and their and society's economic, even democratic well-being. It insists that we devote attention to a highly diverse student body, inside and outside the classroom. It demands that the outcomes of our work not be merely stated, but that they be assessed in terms of students' performance. The public enjoins us to connect explicitly secondary and post-secondary education for maximum educational benefit. But, most importantly, it expects us to do more with less, just as others in the workplace are expected to do. Taken in their aggregate, these forces give greater power over a faculty member's life to the vertical structures of an institution as compared with the horizontal disciplinary pulls and supports for faculty members that, in effect, often remove them from the institution.

As a result, our positioning in the academy now emphasizes our lives as members of the faculty of a department, where that department, for sound academic and sound fiscal reasons, is thought of as a functional entity that offers a certain product, its curriculum, to a wide range of students throughout the University. As a component of a college the department is ideally tied into, and synergistically supportive of a variety of programs, not only in the traditional liberal arts and sciences enterprise, but, increasingly, in a range of professional schools, from business, to engineering, to law, to medicine. Finally, that college may, in turn, be positioned within a university. In order to be able to attract and educate responsibly a definable student population, the university must be able to project a certain institutional mission and identity. Not surprisingly, in the achievement of that goal, it can and does demand certain performance from its faculty, where the judgment of that performance is more than likely to be in terms of institutional priorities, opportunities, and limitations rather than in terms of the judgments of a national, even international disciplinary community.

The implications of such a shift cover the range of possibilities between "to be or not to be," for individual faculty members or entire departments and programs. They are beginning to be translated into new roles which faculty are expected to take on and into new reward structures intended to assure that as many faculty as possible will in fact redirect their energies. The shift, to some extent, can also be detected in university governance and administration; I need only remind you of the TQM movement. And it may really hit us if the discussions by some very thoughtful people were to be put into practice: altering the budgetary behavior of an entire university so as to give primacy to the necessarily collaborative act of delivering a coherent curriculum to students, as contrasted with the current structure which favors individualistic behavior by faculty who, structurally, happen to be arrayed in departments.

These observations may appear not to have any immediate bearing on the future directions of Germanistik. However, I see a direct connection. The question itself, "How visible are we now?," was fortuitously posed by the conference organizers: by putting visibility into the center, it highlights the crucial fact that there is "an other" that is not part of our disciplinary enterprise to whom we must be noticeable and worthy of note, and that that noteworthiness of ours matters since these others may well decide our fate. That kind of a stance contrasts with the assumption underlying past practice that we need primarily to be sufficient unto ourselves. In the case of Germanistik that inherent disciplinary solipsism is even more detrimental because it may not only be constitutionally blind to American realities but inherently constructed as being of superior value. I take the insufficiency of that stance to be at the heart of the wake-up call directed to us by John van Cleve and Leslie Willson in their book.

My answer to "how visible are we now?" depends on the definition of the "we." If we assume a collective "we" for Germanistik in the United States I believe one cannot report anything other than a continued slight downward trend. However, if we define the "we" locally, in terms of "we as a group of faculty in department x in university y" or "we within a city- or state-wide network," positive answers can be provided. I need not give examples here, but there is every indication that the slogan "think globally and act locally" is highly appropriate not only for the nation's economic well-being but also for the well-being of Germanistik in the academy.

Let us quickly remind ourselves of some of the constituencies to whom we should be visible.

1. First and foremost are the *students*, and that, even for college faculty, includes students at the secondary level and even before who are enrolled in German classes, as well as those great numbers whom we never see in our classrooms. As has been pointed out, whatever we can or cannot accomplish at the post-secondary level critically depends on what has been done before. Leaving aside the exciting *Lichtblicke* of some wonderfully innovative immersion programs and K-12 sequences in parts of the country, it is high school language instruction that primarily provides the language abilities of college students. Therefore, it is all the more important for colleges to realize the real danger that the study of German language or, if you will, German Studies, is being crowded out by powerful demographic forces, by a powerful negative reputation for German, and, most importantly, by our complacency toward and even complicity with elitist associations for the study of German. When we complain about high school counselors not recommending German we forget that they are primarily interested in students' success, however ill or shallowly defined. It is a simple fact that we in German generally do not count among those who deliver such success to the overall student population.

From the college's perspective articulation with previous programs becomes critical. Again, by and large, we have shirked from the arduous intellectual and staffing demands of what a true valuation of previous instruction would mean for our curricula. Instead, we have judged previous instruction as deficient, a stance that is all the more curious as it is based on a concept of adult language learning and teaching that is, at the very least, subject to some serious questioning. We continue to take as central those few students who turn into majors, and, within that group of majors particularly those who, ultimately, might become like us, academicians in literature or linguistics.

2. Visibility to *colleagues* in other departments is the next cate-

gory. I am under no illusion about the attendant difficulties. One should not expect open arms, though one might also be surprised at the degree to which collaboration is possible, even welcomed, if and when we think creatively.

3. To accomplish that visibility, a critical component is our ability to position ourselves *within the administration of an institution.* Departmental leadership is crucial here and should be fostered. More than anything else, I believe our future action plan should include the development of politically astute and savvy department chairs. I do not mean here the department chair's ability to keep head above water in the myriad administrative details, nor the requirement that he or she be wonderfully supportive of all colleagues, no matter what their peculiarities. Instead, I am referring to the ability to engage in a hard-nosed analysis of entire institutions, something that too few of us possess. While the likelihood of such a perspective increases with administrative exposure,—and faculty from foreign languages, and German is no exception, generally do not get such exposure—I am also convinced that that perspective is eminently learnable at the department chair level. It involves an ability to understand the implications of an institution's mission and identity, to discern its future directions, particularly in terms of student profile and to relate that profile to programmatic preferences and, therefore, ultimately, to budgetary allocations. It requires a keen sense of an institution's financial situation, its administrative structures, its power relationships, and its budgetary behavior. On the basis of that analysis one can then devise a strategy and develop an action plan with clear goals, with the aim of building up a department from the inside out while constantly referring to its institutional context.

4. Let me close with a final group to whom we must be visible, *the disciplines and the professions.* Lest I be misunderstood, I do not mean the discipline of *Germanistik* but the other disciplines and professions. I realize, of course, that for most of us it is essentially impossible to participate in their internal intellectual discourse. However, it must be possible to gain a sense of their strategic discourse: where do they see their big issues, how do they plan to respond to them on the ground, what initiatives do they engage in as they fend off a public perception that often is not much better than

ours. There is much to learn here, from those who are most closely linked to what we do, for instance from the Classicists and the way in which they have invigorated the study of Latin, or from the initiatives of math and the sciences, begun in the eighties and now in full flowering. We need not track all of them; in all likelihood only some strategic alliances within an institution make sense in any case. But we do need to be perceptive about issues in higher education, at least at the level of insight that a publication like *Change* magazine regularly presents.

How visible we are is a factor of how visible we make ourselves to be. I hope that we, the participants of this conference, will arrive at viable strategies that will provide a general blueprint for action throughout the profession.

7

Present Trends and Future Directions of American Germanics

VALTERS NOLLENDORFS
University of Wisconsin, Madison

I see in the present statistical trends in the profession—a growing feminization and increasing Americanization[1]—a movement toward a much more public and open profession and a movement away from one that is dominated by a group of male expatriate high priests saying their incantations in German and demanding that the congregation respond in German, as has been recently suggested.[2] But I also do not see in these trends the emergence of a unified American Germanics as a method or as a conviction. Personnel changes, ex-

---

[1] Concluding remarks at a forum "On the Future of German at the College and University Level" at the AATG conference at Stanford University 6 August 1995. These remarks were preceded by a presentation of statistical population trends among college and university teachers of German. The main trends indicate (1) that the proportion of women among doctorates has exceeded that of men since 1975 and that it still is growing in the faculty ranks, albeit still with a disproportionate representation in temporary positions; (2) that, though the percentage of German, Austrian, or Swiss-born faculty members is staying relatively stable at just below 40%, the proportion of those with German doctorates is decreasing. The data were obtained by an analysis of data in the DAAD/*Monatshefte* Database. For earlier figures drawn from the Database, see Valters Nollendorfs, "Out of *Germanistik*: Thoughts on the Shape of Things to Come," *Die Unterrichtspraxis* 27 (1994): 6-8.

[2] See John Van Cleve and Leslie Willson, *Remarks on the Needed Reform of German Studies in the United States* (Columbia, SC: Camden House, 1993) 19.

changes, new specializations, proliferating teaching and research methodologies, indeed new methods of instantaneous communication, distance teaching, and research will inevitably bring about changes in our professional demeanor, approach, institutional structure, and policies.

Since I am a believer, however, in conscious consensus building—the nursing along of German Studies in the 1970s and 1980s may be an example—let me suggest some consensus-building ways and directions for guiding these changes and developments:

1. The new discussion begun recently in Frank Trommler's volume *Germanistik in den U.S.A.*,[3] in the *German Quarterly*,[4] *Weimarer Beiträge*,[5] and *Unterrichtspraxis*,[6] in Van Cleve's and Willson's *Remarks on the Needed Reform of German Studies in the United States*,[7] and, yes, continuing in various configurations in *Monatshefte* must go on—in specialized conferences, such as the one held in the fall of 1994 at Vanderbilt University, in our professional meetings, such as this meeting at the AATG conference, and in our publications. Only a *broad* and *continuing* discussion—if need be: debate—can bring about a consensus that will be translated into institutional and organizational action.

2. The goal of such discussion should not be the idea of creating a single "American Germanistic," but rather of establishing a framework for a number of dynamic interactions to occur. Even if we broadly define our main goal and function in North America as interpreters and mediators of German language, literature, and culture, we must not conceive of a ready-made product in whose creation we have no part. Thus the maintenance of close and continuing creative

---

[3] *Germanistik in den USA. Neue Entwicklungen und Methoden*, ed. Frank Trommler (Opladen: Westdeutscher Verlag, 1989).

[4] *The German Quarterly* 62.2 (1989) was devoted to the theme: "Germanistik as German Studies: Interdisciplinary Theories and Methods."

[5] *Weimarer Beiträge* 39.3 (1993).

[6] *Die Unterrichtspraxis* 27.1 (1994) offers focus articles on "German in the 21st Century."

[7] See note 2.

contacts with German-speaking Europe, the acquisition and professional use of the German language, yes_-the intermingling and interaction with colleagues from abroad should be part of this dynamic. This dynamic must, however, not be an intellectual exercise, as it at times threatens to become, but must be conceived in terms of *American educational* policies and needs as they have evolved and are evolving. It must recognize the vast underwater part of our educational iceberg and be based on the premise that each student who once signs up for a high school or college German class is part of our trust and deserves as much attention and care as the brilliant graduate student headed toward a *summa cum laude*. Only if we maintain that ethic can we hope to overcome the perceived malaise in our profession. German Studies, or Germanics, encompass a much wider spectrum of responsibilities than *Germanistik* in German-speaking Europe. Our relationships with our counterparts in German-speaking countries must be informed by this very basic difference. On the other hand, our dynamic must also include creative interaction with American colleagues in disciplines that we must work with in the framework of what we have conceived as German Studies. The use of English in these interactions and in the fulfillment of our broader_- not just German_-community and public functions in America, which we at times have neglected, should be as natural as the use of German and performance of German functions in the other direction. We should listen with both ears and talk out of both sides of our mouths, I hope sensibly and intelligibly. Clearly, I have placed great- _greater_-demands on us than on narrowly defined *Germanistik* in Germany or English and American Studies here, but it must be clear that this cannot and must not be the task of individuals but of individuals cooperating in concert, in consensus, and within a dynamic framework that encompasses all of German teaching from elementary and high school to college and to graduate school.

3. Finally, it would behoove the profession, as it heads into these tasks, to make sure it is informed about itself _ not only about its present shape and future outlook, something I have tried to do with *Monatshefte* Personalia issues, statistical summaries, and the *DAAD/Monatshefte Directory*, but also about its historical heritage

which hides at times surprising revelations about our present short-comings and strengths. A 1996 conference at the University of Wisconsin in Madison will try once again to focus on our recent past.[8] Understanding who we are—Americans, Canadians, Austrians, Swiss, Germans, Britons, a lone Liechtensteinian, and an occasional West and East European, Scandinavian, even a rare Balt and non-European, non-American thrown in—and understanding where we came from academically and professionally may provide guidance for our future discussions and help us develop a new and better sense of identity which will make us no less German but certainly more American in our diversity and in the multiplicity of our missions.

---

[8] A previous attempt was undertaken in the 1980s and resulted in a volume edited by David P. Benseler, Walter F.W. Lohnes, and Valters Nollendorfs, *Teaching German in America: Prolegomena to a History* (Madison: U of Wisconsin P, 1988).

8

On the Undergraduate Curriculum: What's Right / Wrong with It?

Joseph McVeigh
Smith College

Underlying any discussion of a nationwide German (Studies) curriculum is the supposition that such an entity is readily identifiable and quantifiable, that it possesses certain commonalities in all sections of the country. This presumption of something approaching a unified curriculum is in fact symptomatic of a crisis within our profession. In searching for an answer to the question: "What's right or wrong with the undergraduate curriculum in German?"—be it to understand dropping enrollments or to posit a set of approaches to remedy the decline—such scrutiny can only lead at best to partial answers and limited applications. For all those qualities common to undergraduate curricula at large universities and small colleges, at schools with language requirements and those with none, or at schools situated in traditionally ethnic German areas of the country and those with no such demographic base, there are still sufficient variables to render questionable any short assessment such as this. The purpose of this paper, however, is not to raise the question: "What exactly does the American undergraduate curriculum in German look like?" but rather to assume some degree of similarity common to most post-secondary school German (Studies) curricula (i.e. language courses, beginning literature or culture courses, etc.), and to look very briefly at some aspects of this discipline in America which

57

perhaps augur positively for the future and, of course, those which may lie at the base of the steady decline in German enrollments at the undergraduate level.

There are any number of more recent developments in the profession which directly or indirectly enhance the undergraduate experience in German and make it potentially more attractive to American students. Advances in technology, such as satellite dishes capable of receiving direct television transmissions from Germany, or laser-disk programs which bring the tedium of computer-driven exercises to life with visuals, should be utilized to whatever extent they can be effective (certainly in language instruction). Support services, such as the DAAD's database of German Studies curricula, or its funding of professional development workshops, can also have a positive impact on the instructor's preparedness to teach. Similarly, the rich offerings of overseas studies programs complement the curricular menu of American undergraduate institutions and are generally quite popular with students. Certainly, these factors alone do not hold out the prospect of making German more attractive to students. But they cannot be ignored, lest our discipline be perceived as an educational backwater. And the *perception* of our discipline among American students is central to its prospects for growth.

The true dilemma in answering the question posed in the title of this paper is that what might be right at some schools is precisely what's wrong at others! Take for example the current reincarnation of the German curriculum as German Studies, Central European Studies, languages across the curriculum and other such efforts to connect the German curriculum with other disciplines. In principle, and often in practice, this development is a good thing. However, branching out beyond the traditional boundaries of language and literature studies can also bring with it a slow hemorrhaging, the end result of which might be that other departments assume domain over areas which had formerly been considered that of the German (Studies) Department. For example, Germanic mythology or Grimm's fairy tales could be considered quintessentially Germanic in their origins. Yet they are often taught within an English Department as part of genre studies. Courses in Comparative Literature might similarly satisfy a student's curiosity about German culture by reading Kafka,

Mann, Rilke or Brecht in translation. So too, German-language literature dealing with the Holocaust is just as likely to be found today among the offerings of a Jewish Studies program as it is within the curriculum of a German (Studies) Department. In this way, the trend towards diversification is a double-edged sword that could narrow, rather than broaden, our curricular possibilities. Particularly onerous in this respect are programs such as the "Self-Instructed Language Program" (SILP) which implies the superfluousness of language instruction (and instructors) in general. This implication is certainly not lost on college or university administrations who might already eye the study of foreign languages as a mechanical endeavor one step removed from automobile repair.

While we in the profession can think of many reasons why fluency in German and familiarity with the essentials of German culture are valuable goals to pursue, we cannot always sufficiently translate this enthusiasm into increased enrollments in our courses. There are some factors at play here which are more or less beyond our control, and others which we might be able to address. As mentioned above, foreign language departments are often viewed as expendable by administrations looking to save money. The cost of higher education undoubtedly makes many students (not to mention their parents who are footing the bill) focus on courses which are perceived to be more likely to enhance future employment opportunities. But should such factors not play equally on all foreign languages? Logic would dictate that, to varying degrees, they should.

What then is it about the German undergraduate curriculum which has caused its enrollments to stagnate and decline while other foreign languages are, in a relative sense, prospering. The answer, I believe, lies in the perception of the discipline by many undergraduate students who would not be otherwise predisposed to enroll in a German language or culture course, that is, the "undecideds." Quite simply stated, for most young Americans German has no compelling attraction, no "hook," as it were. It has never been perceived as the language of lovers, nor the language of humor, nor the language of high cuisine. It *is*, however, often portrayed and perceived as a harsh idiom of esoteric intellect. Stereotypes of German language and culture as authoritarian, mechanistic and ruthless still abound, thanks to the numbingly redundant efforts of the news and entertainment media.

The image of the German familiar to most college-age American students today is either that of someone to be feared (apart from well-known historical Nazi figures, the Austrian film star Arnold Schwarzenegger embodies this notion in his film role as the robotic "Terminator") or that of the quirky eccentric, such as the figures Hans and Franz or Dieter of the "Saturday Night Live" television show. In short, "German-ness" is at best part of the periphery of what interests most undergraduates: it is the culture and language of highbrow seriousness, which has a tenuous hold at best among many of today's American undergraduates, and of foreboding types such as Hitler or today's skinheads But it is also quite often perceived as a culture of disaffection, alienation and pathology, as personified by Kafka, Nietzsche, and Freud. The perception of German culture among the average uninformed American student runs the gamut from indifference to hostility: "Goethe is boring (it says so in the Book of Lists!); Schiller is a cultural non-entity; Thomas Mann must have been a closet gay because of that Venice thing he wrote. Beethoven—Didn't Hollywood just make a film about his sex life? Mozart—Wasn't he the crazy dude in *Amadeus*? And besides, were the Germans not all Nazis who went into denial after the war? Philosophy ... science ... technology: Einstein was an American, wasn't he?" Stereotypes can be very powerful. Yet, we can never hope to combat them if we cannot draw students into our courses, or even worse, if we unwittingly drive them away by helping to perpetuate the stereotypes.

If the undergraduate German curriculum has a shortcoming that is reflected in the enrollment trends of the last twenty years, it is that the purveyors of this curriculum have been less than stellar in recognizing the forces which have increasingly determined their share of the enrollment pie. Quite simply, we have neither marketed our curriculum well, nor fine-tuned it sufficiently to appeal to its target constituency: American students. The undergraduate has changed over the last 10-20 years both in his/her preparedness for college in general and in his/her perception of things German in particular. The underlying principle of efforts to reverse the effects of this trend cannot be simply structural in nature, i.e. shifting from a literature-based curriculum to inter- or multidisciplinary German Studies. Rather, a core principle of curricular reform must be: "Know your students and what interests them." This may require a bit of field work. German (Studies) instructors may have to seek out students in their various habitats throughout campus, be visible as active members of the campus community, and participate in German Club activities. For as each new generation of undergraduates enters the University, they often bring with them a new set of perceptions and priorities. There have always been, and will likely always be, students who are, for any number of reasons, intellectually fascinated by the rich and varied offerings of German culture. These students we must nurture and challenge to pursue their interests as far as they can.

Nevertheless, there are many undergraduates—indeed, *most* undergraduates—who, despite all efforts, have no such interest and probably never will. The group to which we must direct our attention and resources are the "swing voters" who just might have a general interest in foreign languages and cultures, but no particular reason for selecting one over another. They, like most students who do not have a well-conceived course of study in mind upon entering college, need to be seduced into taking a German language or literature course. And this is where we will probably find our greatest failing: we have not learned to seduce undergraduates to German (Studies), in part because what we have to offer is often a curriculum heavy on the "Angst" and light on the "Fahrvergnügen"; that is, the image of Germany that we offer our campus communities is all too often a somber and uninviting one.

How many students, who, if faced with the choice of attending a "classic" film of the New German Cinema or a popular American film dubbed in German, would not opt for the latter? Audiences in Germany regularly do in huge numbers! Yet many of us still insist that such films are not part of "German culture" and thus unworthy of inclusion into our language curriculum. This crisis of image is exacerbated by problem/issue-oriented readings in language textbooks. What undergraduate has not been fascinated by the wonderfully "interesting" topics such as the German school system, the role of

women in German society, guest workers, etc. While certainly merit-
ing attention at some point, the use of readings on areas such as
these in the early phase of language instruction reinforces the image
of a German culture singularly focused on sociological issues and
problems. Perhaps students are telling us something about this curriculum by voting with their feet. Or perhaps we have the question
backwards. Instead of asking why enrollments have dropped off to a
bit more than 100,000 students today, we might be better served by
asking why the remaining 100,000+ are still interested in German.

If we truly face a crisis of identity in our profession today, we
would do well to examine the motivating factors behind these thousands of souls to see if there is any common ground in their desire to
take German language or culture courses, other than institutional
language requirements or ethnic background. What offerings appear
the most successful in drawing and retaining students within the
German curriculum at various types of schools? What particular aspects of the college or university enhance the possibility of success in
attracting students (e.g. strong German-oriented offerings in other
disciplines such as History, Music, Art History and Political Science)? Are there job- or career-related possibilities that can be better
integrated into our curriculum (e.g. internships)? Does German-
American ethnicity play a role as a motivating factor? If yes, how can
a school's undergraduate German curriculum build on it? How inter-
connected are college-level and secondary-school German curricula
in a particular area? This is a crucial element! The quality and availability of German in the schools will impact for better or worse on
college curricula, since it is in the schools that many of the first impressions are given and reinforced. College and university faculty
should not consider it beneath them to get "down and dirty" in assisting the secondary-school German programs whenever we can. In
this area, the AATG has done an exemplary job of bringing the two
levels together.

In all discussions of our profession and the "crisis" of enrollments, there is rarely, if ever, allusion made to another key element
of the whole equation of enrollment patterns: the faculty. What is
meant here is not professional training, since the undergraduate German (Studies) faculty as a whole is apparently very well trained.

Rather, what is meant are the variables of personality and enthusiasm. In the mix of considerations affecting a student's curricular choices, these elements are often decisive. In private conversations among colleagues in the academy, one regularly hears complaints of "dead wood" which creates a drag on a department; i.e., colleagues unwilling or unable to adjust and adapt to new generations of students. Such colleagues are by no means identifiable solely by age. Equally culpable are some who view undergraduate teaching with disdain, as something that detracts from their scholarly efforts, as if teaching and scholarship were mutually exclusive. Even the best possible German (Studies) curriculum cannot attract and keep students without a lively and engaging faculty doing the teaching.

Can we really learn anything useful about the undergraduate curriculum as a whole that is clearly laudable or just plain lamentable? On the positive side of the balance sheet is an undergraduate curriculum that is quite diverse from school to school across the country, and certainly much more so than twenty years ago. However, that very fact is perhaps symptomatic of our profession's loss of profile, that is, as it became more diverse, it became less popular. One might also raise the question what good it is to offer a large menu of German programs at the undergraduate level if it is only of interest to those precious few who intend to major or minor in German (Studies). For the remaining masses of undergraduates, such diverse offerings often sound too esoteric to attract their interest.

What then might be done to make the undergraduate German (Studies) curriculum more attractive to greater numbers of today's American undergraduates? First, we must familiarize ourselves as individual teachers with any and all creative ideas insofar as they might impact our curriculum. And perhaps we should actually implement some of them as well, taking some risks in creating new courses and programs tailored to today's students. However, we should always be flexible and skeptical enough to dump the innovations if they do not work. Does that sound like an appeal to trendiness? Yes, if by that term one understands the fine-tuning process of matching wavelengths between the suppliers (departments) and consumers (the students). Let the market play a greater role in dictating what aspects of German culture we emphasize—within limits! If a course on German popular culture, for example, could stir interests in other, more "serious" areas of German culture, why not? Such offerings might just provide a needed step in order to mediate to undergraduates the myriad interconnections of German culture. This might, at first, sound like an appeal to "dumb down" the German (Studies) curriculum, but only if one believes certain aspects of German culture in the broadest sense to be inherently "dumb." Likewise, when we reflect as a profession on the undergraduate curriculum we would do well not to get caught up in a theoretical morass of "discourses," as this would only serves to widen the gap between faculty and students. This disjunction lies at the heart of the enrollment problem, for it reveals a dysfunctional aspect of our profession, where our graduate schools prepare generations of teachers to speak an idiom which many, if not most, American undergraduates care little about. We can continue to preach to the faithful few and scratch our heads about apparent student disinterest in things German, or we can take an honest look at the American undergraduate and try to gain some insights that may make us more attractive to them, and more effective as teachers and scholars.

9

Reshaping the Undergraduate Experience in German

DIETER JEDAN
SOUTHEAST MISSOURI STATE UNIVERSITY

I. INTRODUCTION

While the decade of the eighties was dominated by a host of educational reforms relating to the teaching of foreign languages, the nineties appear to focus on enrollments and outcomes assessment.[1] With the overall decline in German enrollments the call is out to restructure programs to attract more students. Declining enrollments in French and German were also the focus of the article in the October 12, 1994 issue of the *Chronicle of Higher Education* entitled, "Spanish, Si! Colleges Report Dramatic Growth in Enrollment; French and German Decline." The authors state that "German, which attracted 146,000 students in 1960 and 202,000 in 1970, had an enrollment of 133,000 in 1990."[2]

The article quotes a foreign language department chairperson, who expresses the sentiment of many a prospective student: "If you

---

[1] See Carl D. Glickman, "Open Accountability for the 90s: Between the Pillars," *Educational Leadership* 47 (1990): 38-42; *Restructuring Schools*, ed. by Richard E. Elmore (San Francisco, CA: Jossey-Bass, 1988); and Michael G. Fullan, *The New Meaning of Educational Change* (New York: Teachers College Press, 1991).

[2] "Spanish, Si! Colleges Report Dramatic Growth in Enrollments," *The Chronicle of Higher Education* (Oct.12'94), A-15.

approach a student about taking French or German, their reaction is, What am I going to do with it?"[3] An Associated Press article published in the *Southeast Missourian* entitled, "Language Classes Popular Among High School Students," quotes a high school student as saying that he is taking Spanish, "a language he chose over German" because he "thought Spanish would help [him] with business in the future."[4] To be sure, there is activity to increase enrollments in foreign languages in general and in German in particular. Yet, there is hesitation as to how this can be achieved at the present time. According to Anne Lewis, "restructuring is a change in 'attitude,' one that recognizes the current system of schooling does not work for a significant number of children and young people and will not provide experiences that ensure excellent opportunities for all young people."[5]

Jobs opportunities and ways to position our programs to take advantage of these opportunities should concern every German language professor who asks himself or herself: "What are our students going to do with German?" and "How can I restructure the program to meet the needs?" Our individual answers to these questions will help us shape the future of our German language and literature programs and then to rethink our current major requirements.

As one of three German instructors in the German section at Southeast Missouri State University, I asked myself these questions upon my arrival in the Fall semester of 1993. At that time, German had one (1) major. Today we have close to two dozen majors. The dramatic growth of our program has implications for other departments. Language faculty in many areas may find that our approach to declining enrollments can help them as well.

II. PURPOSE

The primary purpose of this paper is to discuss my research re-

---

[3] *Chronicle,* A-17.

[4] "Language Classes Popular Among High School Students." *Southeast Missourian,* Monday, November 14, 1994, A7.

[5] Anne Lewis, *Restructuring America's Schools* (Arlington, VA: American Association of School Administrators, 1989), 14.

garding our German program by looking closely at our students and their varying backgrounds. The sources consulted for information about the region where these students come from will also be of interest. By investigating information we have about our students from internal and external sources, inferences can be made about how best to use our resources and where our curricular emphases should be.

In this presentation, I will focus on German, but I would point out that all languages can use some form of my approach to reshape their programs to answer the students' questions as to what they can do with a particular language in the "real world."

To meet the needs of our regional clientele, the Department of Foreign Languages offers French, German, and Spanish language and literature courses, as well as Japanese language classes on a regular basis, and selective other foreign languages, such as Dutch, on occasion. We have major programs for the BA and BS degrees in French, German, and Spanish.

At Southeast, as a direct result of the 1992 Coordinating Board of Higher Education's "Task Force Report," we have begun to redefine the major in foreign languages to expand the range of activities, courses, practica, study abroad courses, international lectures, and internships all of which are now considered appropriate work to meet the criteria for the BA and BS Ed degree requirements. The Task Force Report stated that, "Admission policies of Missouri's public four-year colleges and universities should reinforce and differentiate institution missions in terms of clientele."[6]

During the 1993/94 academic year, the German faculty has struggled to redefine the major in German, to change the focus from literature high-culture to a proficiency-based, communicative skills-oriented approach that would focus on our regional needs as outlined in the Task Force Report.

According to some local international businessmen, our section

[6] "Suggested Statewide Public Policy Initiatives and Goals: Report to the Coordinating Board for Higher Education," *Task Force on Critical Choices for Higher Education.* Adopted June 5, 1992. This citation was taken from "Distinctive Admission Policies."

has in the past represented foreign-language study as just another general education subject intended for cultural enrichment, literary enjoyment, the teaching profession, and for graduate study rather than for meeting the real needs of the business sector as pointed out in the Task Force Report.

With fewer faculty and dwindling resources, departments of foreign languages have to look outside their field to improve the number of majors, the effectiveness of instruction, the quality of the program, and the employability of the graduates.

In the Department of Foreign Languages at Southeast Missouri State University, we have made every effort to find out how the quality and size of the German program can be improved without the immediate need of additional faculty or new resources. Based on my experiences, I will show that the study of German can provide a powerful impetus to the entire liberal arts community, the departments, their service regions, and the business community, because, if done properly, it will free the profession to focus more on improving teaching, updating curricula, educating foreign-language majors for critical areas in business and the professions, and community involvement that draw from the professors' particular expertise.

III. SHAPING OUR FUTURE

While the "Task Force Report" of the Coordinating Board for Higher Education of the State of Missouri set the stage for change by providing all state colleges with "Vision for the Future" statements, I realized early on that change still needed to come from within the individual units. In order to capture the essence of the vision statement, the Department of Foreign Languages wrote its own vision statement.

The administration supported our efforts by requesting state funds in their 1994 budget, outlining specific goals and university-wide needs. Immediately, I began to collect data from the Office of Institutional Research such as the ACT scores of our students, the counties of origin of students enrolled in German and the names of their high schools, if they had taken German on the secondary level. Additionally, data was collected through interviews, surveys, and direct observation to confirm the validity of evidence from the Office of Institutional Research.

On the basis of information gathered the German section made some changes:

(1) The first three semesters of work were combined into two;
(2) A major for German teachers was introduced;
(3) *Deutsche Welle TV* was incorporated into every German course;
(4) High school teachers in the region received video copies of *Deutsche Welle TV*;
(5) An internship program for German majors in local international companies was initiated;
(6) Began a German film series;
(7) Inaugurated an international lecture series; some lectures were in the foreign language with simultaneous interpretation;
(8) Chartered an honors society;
(9) Hosted a weekly TV talk show *International Crossroads*;
(10) Offered an AP summer course for high school teachers;
(11) Invited high school teachers to bring students to our campus;
(12) Started a Foreign Language Fair with academic competitions to encourage students to continue their FL studies;
(13) Offered affordable study trips to Germany for under $ 1,000.00;
(14) Began evening classes in German to attract non-traditional students;
(15) Involved the community in our discussions; and
(16) Began planning dual-credit options whereby high school students could also earn college credit while taking high school German.

My discussions with high school German teachers and local business leaders documented the need for more outreach programs such as lectures, films, and video programs to bring to the fore the importance of foreign languages in the global marketplace. These discussions also brought home the need to share with our colleagues on the high school level relevant articles dealing with employment, teaching methodology, internships, and the like.

An article which appeared in *The Wall Street Journal* entitled "Glut of Graduates Lets Recruiters Pick Only the Best" undergirded our efforts by pointing out that "companies can now demand skills they didn't even hope for in the past. Some are looking for better grades, while others, expanding overseas and selling to more diverse customers at home, are focusing on candidates who are fluent in at least one foreign language."[7] We can equip students with these skills only when the high schools and colleges work together. Also, my observations in the high schools documented the need for more in-service methods courses and for more interaction between high-school students enrolled in German and our college students to encourage the former to continue their language studies after graduation.

Furthermore, I also researched the service region by:

(1) Speaking with regional businessmen whose companies had international ties; and by (2) studying the results of the most recent US Census regarding such topics as:
(a) What is the per capita income in our region?
(b) What proportion of the population has a high school diploma?
(c) What is the educational attainment of the population that is over 25?
(d) Numbers of degrees granted in various majors in the region?
(e) What are the occupations of the employed persons in the region?
(f) What is the projected annual growth in employment by industry between 1990 to 2000?
(g) What percentage of adults in the region have literacy problems?

With the data from our Office of Institutional Research, the results of my interviews and observations, and the wealth of information from the 1990 US Census as well as other sources, I looked anew

[7] "Glut of Graduates Lets Recruiters Pick Only the Best," *The Wall Street Journal* (May 20, 1993), B-1.

at our (A) program in German; (B) our region; and (C) ways of meeting the needs of both.

A. 1990-1995 Situational Analysis of the Foreign Language Programs

A cursory look at the data from the Office of Institutional Research offered me a wealth of information ranging from enrollment numbers to ACT scores, from ethnic background to grades, from home high school to naming the county where the family resides. A faculty member who is interested in finding out what type of students have been enrolled in a program is, therefore, well-advised to look at these data before making any changes in the curriculum. (TABLES I-III) My findings had implications for what types of outreach programs should be offered, their cost, and for our recruiting strategies.

B. Situational Analysis of the Region

Like the wealth of information that is available to the faculty member from the Office of Institutional Research at Southeast Missouri State University, there is a similar wealth of information for the region easily accessible and available from the US Census Bureau.

When mapping a Department's potential, hard figures from such sources can provide "reality checks" necessary to stay focused. I felt that the US Census information might be helpful in planning our approach to charting our involvement in the region and to make sure that our resources will be used most effectively.

Using US Census data, I was able able to paint a clearer picture of our region: (1) needs and per capita income; (2) counties with the highest population rate of persons with less than a high school education; (3) the educational attainments of the population; (4) a listing of baccalaureate degrees granted in the region; (5) the occupations of all employed persons in the region; (6) future employment trends; (7) percentage of the population with literacy problems and their locations.

A professor seeking to devise a model foreign-language program is well advised to use these US Census data in conjuction with the other available information, to observe all levels of FL classes in the high schools, to talk to high school teachers in the regional feeder high schools, and to meet with regional employers to find out what kinds of foreign-language skills are critical. The US Census data only provides an overall view while the other sources provide the context.

To follow the dictates of the CBHE "Task Force Report" and to initiate curricular reform in German at Southeast, I also analyzed data from our region looking specifically at US Census data to develop long-term strategies for enrollment growth. Some of the information proved particularly useful in my efforts:

    a. Per capita income in the service region;
    b. What percentage has high school education;
    c. What is the educational attainment of the population;
    d. What is the proportion of BA/BS degrees granted in the region;
    e. Occupations of employment;
    f. Projected annual growth of employment and occupations of employed persons;
    g. What regions in the service regions have literacy problems.

These data, when combined with those from our Office of Institutional Research, the goals of the university, of the various colleges within the university, and the vision statement of the CBHE Task Force Report, provided additional direction planning our outreach programs, degree requirements, and experiential learning experiences. Figures 1-7 present my findings in a more graphic fashion (see end of chapter).

C. Meeting the Needs of the Program and the Region

Based on the data, we felt that direct involvement in the region was important. We wanted to involve not only the students and the other departments within the University but also the community and the regional feeder high schools in our programs and activities. We achieved this goal by offering a host of programs in all languages. The most noticeable changes occured nearly overnight when the Department began to offer an array of opportunities. They bear repeating:

(1) German TV (via satellite);

(2) A lecture series entitled "Travel Abroad at Home" which offers free lunches and interesting lectures some of which are simultaneously interpreted;

(3) A weekly TV talkshow entitled "International Crossroads" hosted by a foreign language major offers perspectives on global events. Experts on the programs are our FL majors;

(4) An internship program for foreign language majors with local companies where foreign languages are used;

(5) Foreign films in German (and other foreign languages). The Department offers between 50 and 60 movies in French, German, and Spanish each academic year;

(6) Inexpensive study abroad opportunities; our students can spend two weeks overseas for $ 995.00;

(7) Student research opportunities with faculty;

(8) Free daily tutoring in German with native speakers;

(9) An academic Foreign Language Fair;

(10) Free video copies from *Deutsche Welle TV* for high school teachers and their students.

With the increase in programs and activities came an increase in enrollment in German. A look at the number of majors in History showed that our increase in majors was not matched by similar increases in other departments during the same two-year period. In fact, when looking at the the overall enrollment of the university which had declined by about 10% during the same period, it became obvious that our work was paying off.

Since the per capita income of the residents in our service region is slightly higher than $ 9,000.00 per year (see Fig.1) most of our students are half- or full-time employed to pay for their education at Southeast. This also meant that for our study-abroad programs to be attractive, they must be affordable, preferably under $ 1,000.00. We achieved this goal within the first year.

The educational attainment of persons in our service region who are older than 25 years shows that 20% have an 8th grade education or less, 35% have high school diplomas, and less than 20% have some kind of college background. Assuming that these are the parents of some of our students in foreign languages, the Department wanted to offer a variety of programs (films, lectures, trips) to stimulate interest in international issues, overseas study, and foreign-language study.

Many of the adults have basic literacy problems in our service region (l3% to 15% (see Fig.7). It is unlikely that many of the students are exposed to global viewpoints at home. Indeed, literacy needs to be taken into consideration in everything we do. As a result, we decided to make available copies of *Deutsche Welle TV* not only to regional high school teachers, but also to their students and parents. We felt that this program would bring up-to-date material into the high-school German classroom, thus improving the quality of instruction while maintaining student interest.

On campus, we began to introduce live TV (by satellite) to all dormitory units to bring multicultural issues, cultural literacy, and current international information to the foreign-language student and campus community. We also decided to send copies of these programs to all foreign language teachers in the region to improve the quality of instruction of the students even before they come to our classes.

Projected population changes between now and 2020 indicated that our region is well above the state and St. Louis area averages. With the rise in international companies moving to our service region, we argued, the university was well advised to prepare the future graduate for a global market right here in Southern Missouri.

The occupations of presently employed persons in our service region indicated that the manufacture of precision products leads the region, with administrative/executive/managerial and teachers/counselors in second and third place, respectively. With the expected growth in international companies, our Department was well advised to meet with the faculty of our College of Industry and with representatives of corporations to determine how we can help to meet their present and future needs.

Interesting was the projected annual growth in employment by industry to the year 2000. The Southeast service region again is projected to lead in the growth of manufacturing, retail, and service jobs (see Figs. 5,6).

Only about 3% of all baccaraureate degrees granted by universities in the Southeast service region list foreign languages as a major. With well over 100 companies with international business connections in our 100-mile service region radius, we felt that there was a real need for foreign-language professionals out there. Our job was to inform our students about these jobs to allow them at an early stage in their career to combine a major in, for example, German and a pre-professional specialization, such as international business, criminal justice, nursing, journalism, mass communication, political science, drafting, engineering, and accounting (see Fig.4).

IV. Rethinking Our Mission

The results of our regional analysis, the nine objectives of Southeast's School of University Studies, and the CBHE. Task Force Report provided a general framework of what our students need to meet the present and future needs of the university, the regional employers, and the profession.

How did our program change as a result over the past years? To the outsider, probably not very much except for the outreach activities. Early in the academic year, the department adopted proficiency levels which our students must attain in order to graduate with a foreign-language major. The ACTFL guidlines were accepted to povide a sound basis for assessing the linguistic skills area although we developed our own descriptors for the proficiency levels.

Additionally, we agreed to accept only those students into our major program who go through entrance, mid-point, and exit interviews. While the entrance interview in the foreign language was for purposes of selection, the mid-point interview was for diagnostic purposes, and the exit interview was for quality control. A Portfolio requirement was also instituted, requesting that all majors provide a portfolio of their work at the time of the mid-point and exit interviews.

The most obvious and exciting changes in our department happened, however, outside the formal curriculum, in our offerings of lectures, films, satellite TV, international study programs, and internship opportunities. As a result of our efforts, the Department of Foreign Languages has become a cultural and intellectual leader on the Southeast campus and in the community. What follows is a list of our activities.

1. ADVANCED PLACEMENT WORKSHOPS

To meet the CBHE Task Force Report goal to have an AP Program in every Missouri school, our department decided to offer an annual summer AP workshop for high school teachers of foreign languages.

2. TRAVEL ABROAD AT HOME

This is the title of our lecture series which brings to the campus a variety of lecturers, slide presentations, and colloquia to provide the campus community with information about the world around us. Some lectures are given in the target language (usually one per language per semester) which are simultaneously translated into English. To make this lecture even more attractive we offer free pizza and coke (average attendance is 50).

3. FOREIGN TRAVEL

"Christmas in Germany" and "Summer in Memmingen" provide our students with inexpensive, two week travel opportunities overseas. Neither of these trips cost more than $ 995.00 which includes airfare, hotel, two meals, all trips in the country, and admission fees. This past summer 15 persons participated. "Sojourn in a Castle" is intended to raise funds for scholarships. This program is geared toward alumni who are willing to donate $ 500.00 in addition to the cost of the trip.

4. FACULTY-STUDENT RESEARCH

All faculty in the Department are encouraged to share their research with our majors, to provide them with learning opportunities outside the classroom, to work with them on research projects, and to co-present scholarly papers at conferences locally, regionally, and nationally. During the 1993/94 academic year six of our majors (two from each language) traveled with two professors to Wisconsin to present a paper.

5. INTERNATIONAL FILM SERIES

Each semester, the Department shows an average of 20 to 25 foreign films with English subtitles. These films are in French, German, and Spanish and provide our students and community a glimpse into the culture and language not normally available in the classroom setting. The average attendance is about 40 for French, 30 for German, and 35 to 40 for Spanish.

6. FREE DAILY TUTORING SERVICE

The Department provides daily tutoring services for students in French, German, and Spanish. Since German is least likely to be offered in our regional high schools, two hours of daily tutoring is offered to German students to provide for maximum exposure. Students can come to the tutor to talk, to discuss their assignments, or just to ask questions about their class work.

7. INTERNATIONAL TV (BY SATELLITE)

During the 1993 Fall semester, we applied for a grant to install international TV in our foreign-language classroom building and to connect all student dormitories by cable to this service. The first foreign TV programs were aired in late October 1993.

8. EXPERIENTIAL LEARNING

As part of our beginning foreign-language course requirements we are asking our students to visit local and regional companies with international ties to learn what types of skills the companies currently require.

9. INTERNSHIPS

As a result of our very active lecture series we now have two internship possibilities. Presently, we are working on the internship rules and guidelines to ensure a better match between student and employer.

10. RESOURCE CENTER FOR HIGH SCHOOL TEACHERS

In order to improve the next generation of foreign-language students, we have begun to provide area high schools with free copies of our foreign TV programs received by satellite. During the past academic year we distributed well over 250 hours of programming. The first tape is provided free of charge. It is hoped that teachers will return the tape for new material thereafter. Copying and postage is free.

11. FOREIGN-LANGUAGE FAIR

We began an academic foreign-language fair to stress the importance of academics and to allow high school students to compare programs and to bring students to campus for recruitment purposes. Last year 12 schools with over 300 students attended.

12. PRACTICAL LEARNING

We encourage local companies who have translation needs to hire our majors. The translations are supervised by a faculty member and the work is included in the student's portfolio.

13. COMMUNITY OUTREACH

All our activities are open to the community. Community members can also join us on our foreign study trips provided they meet the same requirements. This past summer a number of community people traveled with my group to Germany. Upon their return some have indicated that they would like to make a donation to our scholarship funds to help Southeast students experience the foreign culture.

14. TV TALKSHOW "INTERNATIONAL CROSSROADS"

Finally, our department began to offer our majors one additional experiential learning opportunity by starting a weekly talkshow which is hosted by one of our majors.

V. Conclusions

We must not only know our past in order to move ahead in our programs, we must also address our region's unique and critical needs. These needs can be met most effectively when we research this topic with the same vigor and depth we research our professional presentations and literary papers. In the past, departments represented foreign-language study as just another general education subject taught for cultural enrichment, literary enjoyment, or graduate study. To ensure the future of our profession, we must seek to combine these with the real needs of our service region, the mission of the university, and the job market.

Few developments in higher education at Southeast have received as much attention as our attempts to expand the traditional FL curriculum by incorporating the needs of the community at large.We have gone a long way in sensitizing our region to the value of foreign languages and the global nature of the job market.

The short-term and long-term implications of our programs, in my opinion, will be far-reaching. Aside from the increased numbers of majors, there will be more community support for foreign-language study on all levels, more company interest in our foreign-language interns, and more majors traveling overseas. With regard to our curriculum, our changes have positioned our Department to play a significant role in the future cross-listing of high school/college courses and programs, encouraging cooperative ventures with regional businesses, and emphasizing ties between the region and the Department. The expected curricular changes will have a lasting effect on the shape of undergraduate education in general.

The important role played by foreign languages in its regional context should not be ignored by other departments. In her article, "Studying the Tangled Bank," Betty Jean Craige touches upon this subject, calling for a re-linking of languages and literatures with their social contexts,[8] because learning a foreign language involves more than the mere acquiring of a skill. Heidi Byrnes argues that "language learning involves not only acquiring a skill but becoming a different person."[9] And the latter involves everyone: the students, the parents,

[8] Betty Jean Craige, "Studying the Tangled Bank," *ADFL Bulletin* 22.2 (1991): 25-28.

[9] Heidi Byrnes, "Foreign Language Departments and the Cultural Component of an International Studies Program," *ADFL Bulletin* 22.1 (1991): 10-15.

the region, the high schools, the regional businesses, the college faculty, the Department, and the University.[10]

[10] Information for this paper was also received from the Office of Institutional Research, Southeast Missouri State University, the US Census Bureau, the 1990 US Census, and from the National Center for Educational Statistics/Integrated Postsecondary Education Data Systems (NCES/-IPEDS), Office of Education, Washington, DC. I would like to express my gratitude to the Librarians of Kent Library, Southeast Missouri State University and the City of Cape Girardeau Library for their assistance in locating some of the information.

Table 1

NOTES: 1) 4th week census data. Double majors are tallied in each major.
2) Characteristics are from the most recent semester of enrollment within an academic year.

Southeast Missouri State University
Office of Institutional Research
04MAY95

UNDERGRADUATE MAJORS
PART 1: DEPARTMENT TOTALS

COLLEGE OF LIBERAL ARTS AND DEPT: FOREIGN LANGUAGE		ACADEMIC YEAR				
		90/91	91/92	92/93	93/94	94/95
ALL MAJORS		44	41	38	50	58
CREDIT HOURS		948	887	967	1,073	1,143
FTE		763	692	869	775	835
LOAD						
PARTTIME		22	19	10	26	34
FULLTIME		22	22	28	24	24
..CLASS LEVEL DIST..						
BEG FRESH		.	.	1	.	1
FRESHMAN		2	3	4	5	2
SOPHOMORE		3	7	4	7	13
JUNIOR		20	12	11	12	13
SENIOR		18	18	18	25	28
2D DEGREE		1	1	.	1	1
..GENDER/ETHNICITY..						
FEMALE	CAUCN AM	31	33	25	32	37
	NR ALIEN	1	1	2	3	1
	AFRIC AM	1	.	.	.	.
	HISPC AM	.	.	.	.	1
	ASIAN AM	2	.	.	.	1
	TOTAL	35	34	27	35	40
MALE	CAUCN AM	8	6	8	10	11
	NR ALIEN	.	1	3	5	4
	AFRIC AM	.	.	.	.	2
	HISPC AM	.	.	.	.	1
	NATIV AM	1	.	.	.	.
	TOTAL	9	7	11	15	18
..AVG AGE..	BEG FRESH	.	.	18.2	.	47.0
	FRESHMAN	18.7	18.5	18.9	19.1	18.5
	SOPHOMORE	22.5	21.0	20.3	23.5	20.2
	JUNIOR	25.1	23.7	21.5	21.7	23.3
	SENIOR	26.8	28.9	27.2	25.3	23.2
	2D DEGREE	26.8	27.8	.	24.8	36.7
	ALL	25.4	25.3	23.7	23.6	23.0
HS CLASS PCTL	AVG	77.4	78.0	76.1	73.8	71.9
HS GPA	AVG	3.14	3.21	3.27	3.33	3.26
CUM GPA	AVG	3.04	3.21	3.13	3.00	2.98
..ACT COMP..						
NOTST	%	6.8	9.8	13.2	18.0	17.2
01-16	%	2.3	.	.	.	1.7
17-18	%	4.5	2.4	2.6	2.0	3.4
19-23	%	43.2	41.5	44.7	28.0	31.0
24-27	%	22.7	29.3	21.1	32.0	25.9
28-32	%	20.5	17.1	18.4	20.0	17.2
33-36	%	.	.	.	.	3.4
AVG		23.9	24.2	23.8	24.5	24.1
N		41	37	33	41	48
..ACT ENGL..						
NOTST	%	6.8	12.2	15.8	20.0	17.2
01-12	%	.	.	.	.	1.7
13-19	%	4.5	2.4	7.9	6.0	8.6
20-24	%	29.5	26.8	26.3	26.0	29.3
25-29	%	29.5	31.7	31.6	30.0	24.1
30-36	%	29.5	26.8	18.4	18.0	19.0
AVG		26.8	26.9	26.2	25.9	25.1
N		41	36	32	40	48
..ACT MATH..						
NOTST	%	6.8	12.2	15.8	20.0	17.2
01-16	%	15.9	12.2	13.2	6.0	12.1
17-18	%	2.3	4.9	7.9	6.0	8.6
19-23	%	54.5	46.3	42.1	44.0	36.2
24-27	%	15.9	17.1	7.9	18.0	20.7
28-32	%	2.3	4.9	7.9	4.0	3.4
33-36	%	2.3	2.4	5.3	2.0	1.7
AVG		21.2	21.9	22.2	22.2	21.7
N		41	36	32	40	48

Table 2

NOTES: 1) 4th week census data. Double majors are tallied in each major.
2) Characteristics are from the most recent semester of enrollment within an academic year.
Southeast Missouri State University
Office of Institutional Research
04MAY95

UNDERGRADUATE MAJORS
PART 2: MAJOR COMPARISON

COLLEGE OF LIBERAL ARTS
AND DEPT: FOREIGN LANGUAGE

		ACADEMIC YEAR				
		90/91	91/92	92/93	93/94	94/95
..HEADCOUNT..						
FRENCH		19	12	12	12	13
GERMAN		.	.	1	14	19
SPANISH		25	29	25	24	26
..CREDIT HOURS..						
FRENCH		449	240	320	259	301
GERMAN		.	.	27	262	378
SPANISH		499	647	620	552	464
..FTE..						
FRENCH		397	168	314	189	267
GERMAN		.	.	28	153	282
SPANISH		366	525	526	432	285
..LOAD..						
FRENCH	PARTTIME	8	6	2	6	5
	FULLTIME	11	6	10	5	8
GERMAN	PARTTIME	.	.	.	10	10
	FULLTIME	.	.	1.	4	9
SPANISH	PARTTIME	14	13	8	10	19
	FULLTIME	11	16	17	14	7
..CLASS LEVEL DIST..						
FRENCH	FRESHMAN	2	.	2	1	1
	SOPHOMORE	1	3	2	2	1
	JUNIOR	10	4	3	2	4
	SENIOR	6	5	5	6	7
	2D DEGREE	.	.	.	1	.
GERMAN	BEG FRESH	.	.	.	.	1
	FRESHMAN	.	.	.	1	.
	SOPHOMORE	.	.	.	5	6
	JUNIOR	.	.	.	4	6
	SENIOR	.	.	1	4	6
SPANISH	BEG FRESH	.	.	1	.	.
	FRESHMAN	.	3	2	3	1
	SOPHOMORE	2	4	2	.	6
	JUNIOR	10	8	8	6	3
	SENIOR	12	13	12	15	15
	2D DEGREE	1	1	.	.	1
..GENDER..						
FRENCH	FEMALE	15	10	10	10	11
	MALE	4	2	2	2	2
GERMAN	FEMALE	.	.	.	9	10
	MALE	.	.	1	5	9
SPANISH	FEMALE	20	24	17	16	19
	MALE	5	5	8	8	7
..ETHNICITY..						
FRENCH	CAUCN AM	18	12	11	10	11
	NR ALIEN	.	.	1	2	1
	AFRIC AM	1	.	.	.	1
GERMAN	CAUCN AM	.	.	1	13	17
	NR ALIEN	.	.	.	1	1
	AFRIC AM	.	.	.	.	1
SPANISH	CAUCN AM	21	27	21	19	20
	NR ALIEN	1	2	4	5	3
	HISPC AM	.	.	.	.	2
	ASIAN AM	2	.	.	.	1
	NATIV AM	1	.	.	.	.
..HS CLASS PCTL..						
FRENCH	AVG	75.9	72.4	75.8	79.0	78.1
GERMAN	AVG	.	.	95.7	68.8	68.0
SPANISH	AVG	78.8	80.7	78.2	74.9	71.3
..HS GPA..						
FRENCH	AVG	3.15	3.16	3.01	3.36	3.22
GERMAN	AVG	.	.	4.00	3.26	3.17
SPANISH	AVG	3.13	3.23	3.34	3.35	3.34
..CUM GPA..						
FRENCH	AVG	2.93	3.04	3.10	3.05	3.03
GERMAN	AVG	.	.	2.94	2.93	2.78
..CUM GPA..						
SPANISH	AVG	3.13	3.28	3.16	3.02	3.09
..ACT COMP..						
FRENCH	AVG	24.1	25.3	24.7	25.5	25.5
GERMAN	AVG	.	.	25.0	24.4	23.8
SPANISH	AVG	23.7	23.8	23.2	24.1	23.6
..ACT ENGL..						
FRENCH	AVG	27.9	29.5	28.1	26.5	27.3
GERMAN	AVG	.	.	25.0	25.8	24.3
SPANISH	AVG	25.8	25.8	25.2	25.6	24.5
..ACT MATH..						
FRENCH	AVG	20.8	21.5	22.1	23.5	23.3
GERMAN	AVG	.	.	31.0	21.8	20.9
SPANISH	AVG	21.5	22.1	21.8	21.8	21.4

Table 3

NOTES: 1) 4th week census data. Double majors are tallied in each major.
2) Characteristics are from the most recent semester of enrollment within an academic year.
Southeast Missouri State University
Office of Institutional Research
04MAY95

UNDERGRADUATE MAJORS
PART 1: DEPARTMENT TOTALS

COLLEGE OF LIBERAL ARTS
AND DEPT: HISTORY

		ACADEMIC YEAR				
		90/91	91/92	92/93	93/94	94/95
ALL MAJORS		154	179	191	160	165
CREDIT HOURS		3,069	3,943	4,022	3,891	3,599
FTE		2,197	3,208	2,925	3,410	2,836
LOAD						
PARTTIME		87	79	104	55	76
FULLTIME		67	100	87	105	89
..CLASS LEVEL DIST..						
BEG FRESH		.	1	2	2	.
FRESHMAN		30	35	32	18	19
SOPHOMORE		29	49	52	38	35
JUNIOR		34	34	58	43	42
SENIOR		48	49	38	52	62
2D DEGREE		12	10	8	7	7
DUAL ENRL		1	1	1	.	.
..GENDER/ETHNICITY..						
FEMALE	CAUCN AM	63	77	87	74	85
	NR ALIEN	.	.	.	.	1
	AFRIC AM	.	.	1	2	3
	TOTAL	63	77	88	76	89
MALE	CAUCN AM	84	98	94	82	75
	NR ALIEN	.	.	1	.	.
	AFRIC AM	5	1	5	2	1
	HISPC AM	.	1	1	.	.
	ASIAN AM	1	1	1	.	.
	NATIV AM	1	1	1	.	.
	TOTAL	91	102	103	84	76
..AVG AGE..	BEG FRESH	.	31.1	18.1	21.2	.
	FRESHMAN	19.6	20.4	19.7	19.1	20.8
	SOPHOMORE	22.7	22.7	22.5	20.7	21.7
	JUNIOR	24.5	23.5	23.4	23.6	24.2
	SENIOR	27.7	25.3	25.3	25.3	25.1
	2D DEGREE	34.5	37.2	36.1	28.5	32.6
	DUAL ENRL	23.8	40.2	23.6	.	.
	ALL	25.0	24.0	23.4	23.1	24.0
HS CLASS PCTL	AVG	67.5	67.8	67.9	70.3	74.6
HS GPA	AVG	2.95	3.11	3.11	3.20	3.28
CUM GPA	AVG	2.75	2.80	2.78	2.88	2.96
..ACT COMP..						
NOTST	%	13.6	14.5	15.2	15.0	15.8
01-16	%	0.6	1.7	2.6	2.5	0.6
17-18	%	6.5	2.8	5.8	6.3	4.6
19-23	%	45.5	42.5	41.4	35.0	32.7
24-27	%	23.4	26.3	22.0	27.5	30.3
28-32	%	10.4	12.3	13.1	13.8	15.2
33-36	%	.	.	.	.	0.6
AVG		23.0	23.3	23.1	23.5	24.0
N		133	153	162	136	139
..ACT ENGL..						
NOTST	%	14.9	15.6	15.2	15.0	15.8
01-12	%	.	.	0.5	.	0.6
13-19	%	18.2	21.2	23.0	21.9	15.8
20-24	%	32.5	30.2	30.9	26.9	24.2
25-29	%	28.6	26.8	24.1	28.1	34.5
30-36	%	5.8	6.1	6.3	8.1	9.1
AVG		23.1	23.2	23.0	23.4	24.1
N		131	151	162	136	139
..ACT MATH..						
NOTST	%	14.9	15.6	15.2	15.0	15.8
01-16	%	16.9	18.4	19.9	15.0	10.3
17-18	%	13.6	10.6	14.1	15.6	14.5
19-23	%	41.6	38.5	33.5	35.0	37.6
24-27	%	9.7	10.6	12.6	11.3	14.5
28-32	%	3.2	6.1	4.7	7.5	6.1
33-36	%	.	.	.	0.6	1.2
AVG		20.0	20.3	20.0	20.6	21.2
N		131	151	162	136	139

83

Figure 1

PER CAPITA INCOME OF RESIDENTS IN SEMO SERVICE AREA
(1989)

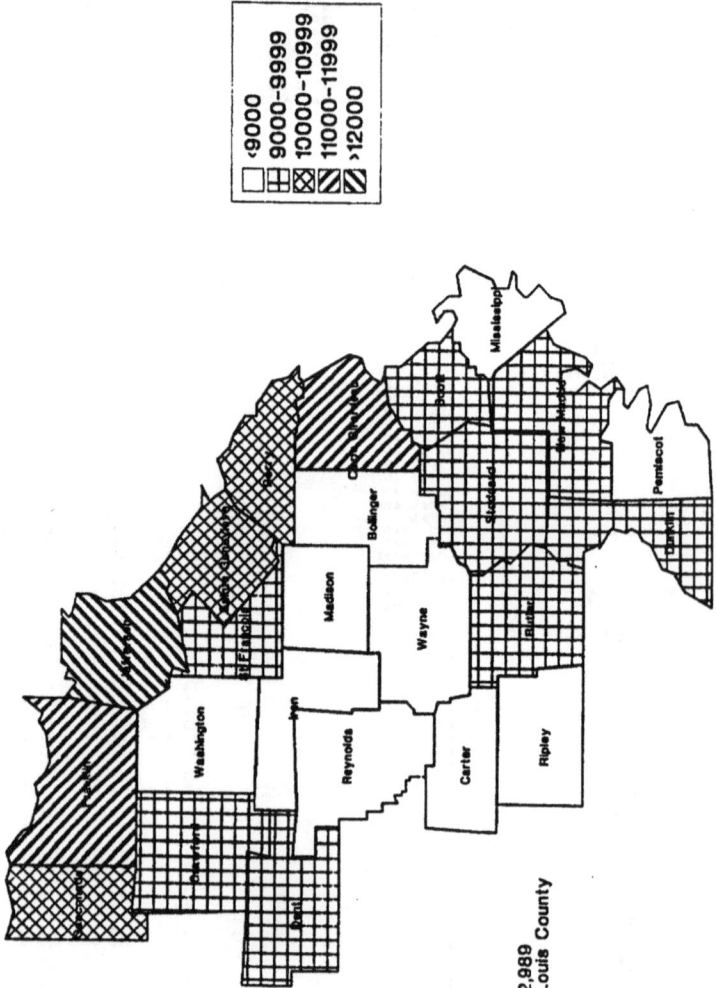

Legend:
- <9000
- 9000–9999
- 10000–10999
- 11000–11999
- >12000

Note: Statewide average = 12,989
Exceeded only by St. Louis County

Source: U.S. Census Bureau

Figure 2

Source: U.S. Census, 1990

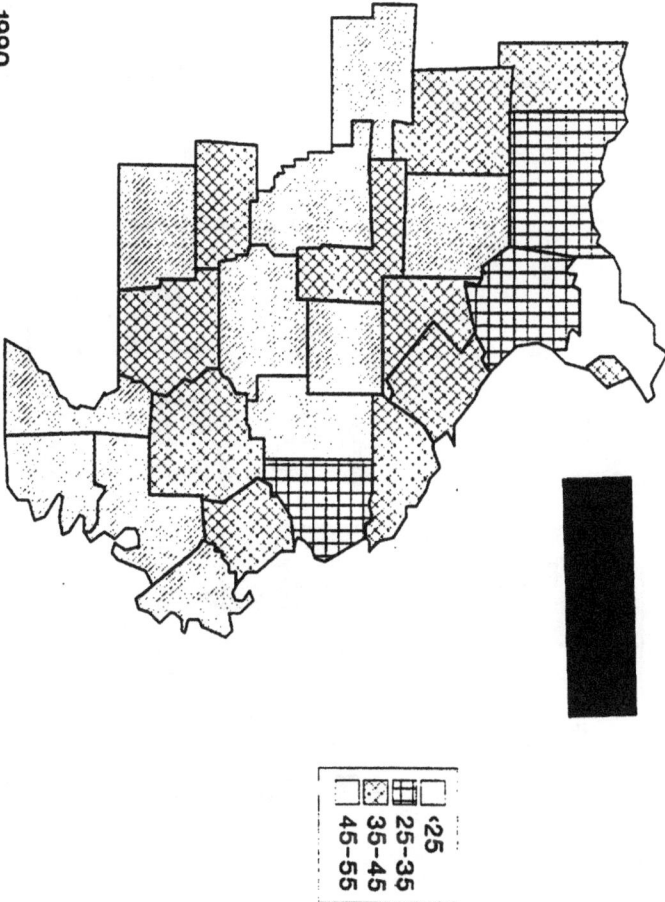

PROPORTION OF POPULATION AGE 25 AND OLDER
WITH LESS THAN A HIGH SCHOOL EDUCATION

<25
25-35
35-45
45-55

85

Figure 3

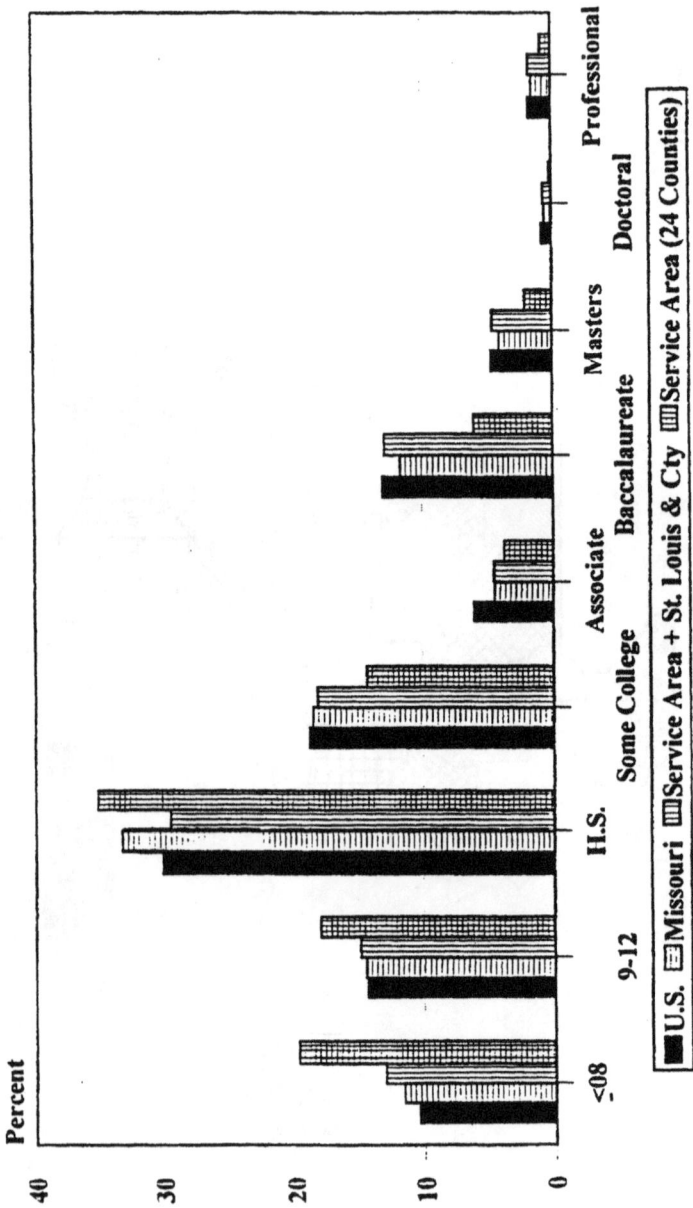

EDUCATIONAL ATTAINMENT OF THE POPULATION
25 AND OLDER

Percent

U.S.   Missouri   Service Area + St. Louis & Cty   Service Area (24 Counties)

<08   9-12   H.S.   Some College   Associate   Baccalaureate   Masters   Doctoral   Professional

Figure 4

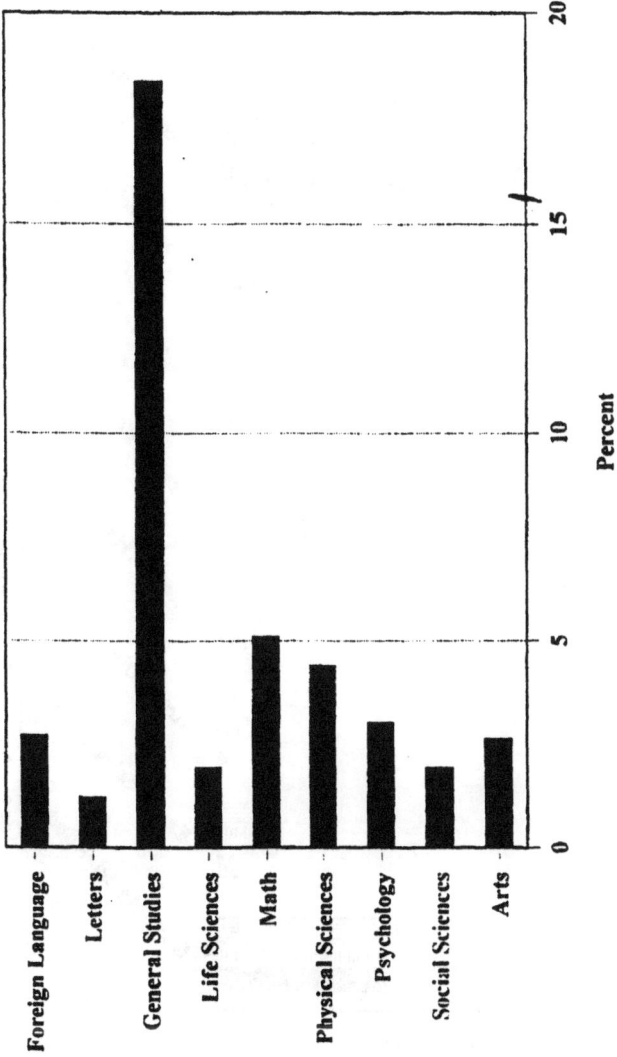

GRANTED BY UNIVERSITIES IN SEMO SERVICE AREA

Foreign Language
Letters
General Studies
Life Sciences
Math
Physical Sciences
Psychology
Social Sciences
Arts

0   5   10   15   20

Percent

Source: NCES, IPEDS 1991 .

Figure 5

OCCUPATIONS OF EMPLOYED PERSONS, 1990

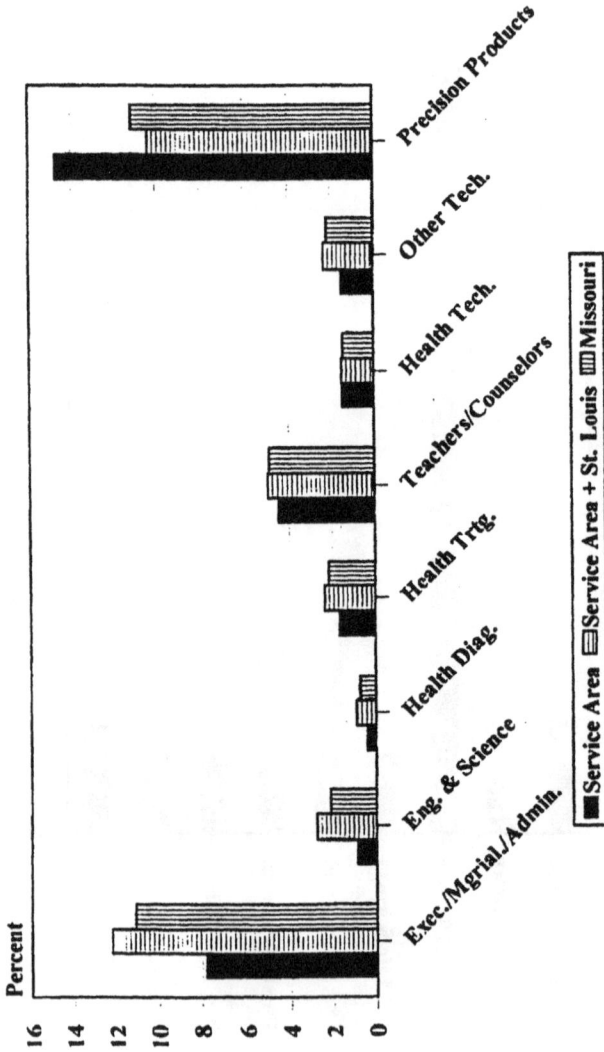

Percent

Legend: ■ Service Area ▥ Service Area + St. Louis ▨ Missouri

Source: U.S. Census, 1990

Figure 6

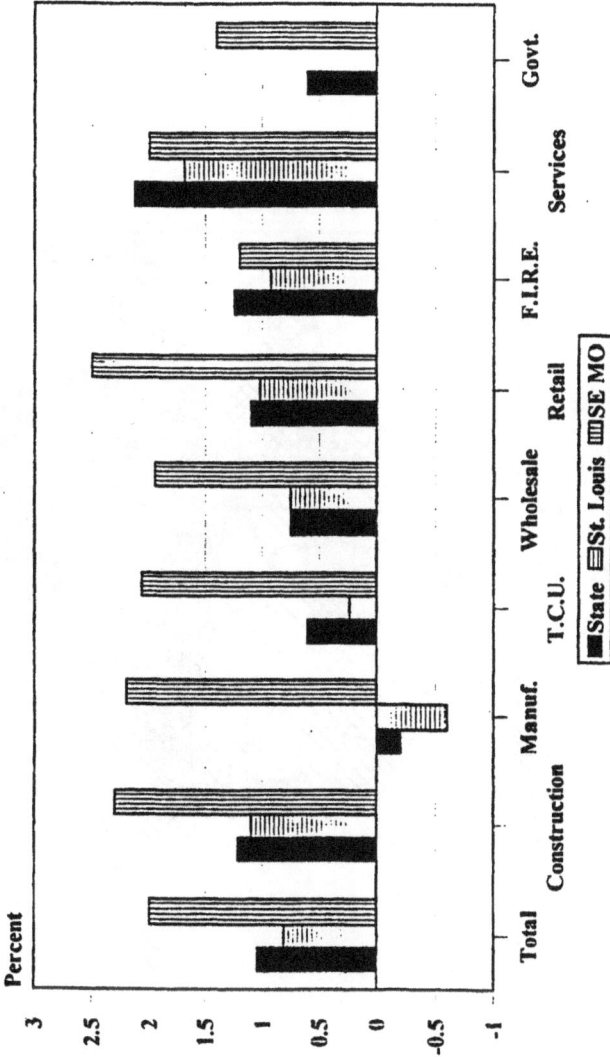

PROJECTED ANNUAL GROWTH IN EMPLOYMENT,
BY INDUSTRY - 1990-2000

Percent

Total   Construction   Manuf.   T.C.U.   Wholesale   Retail   F.I.R.E.   Services   Govt.

■ State   ▤ St. Louis   ▥ SE MO

Source: Employment Outlook, Projections to 2000

89

Figure 7

Estimated Percent of Adults
With Basic Literacy Problems

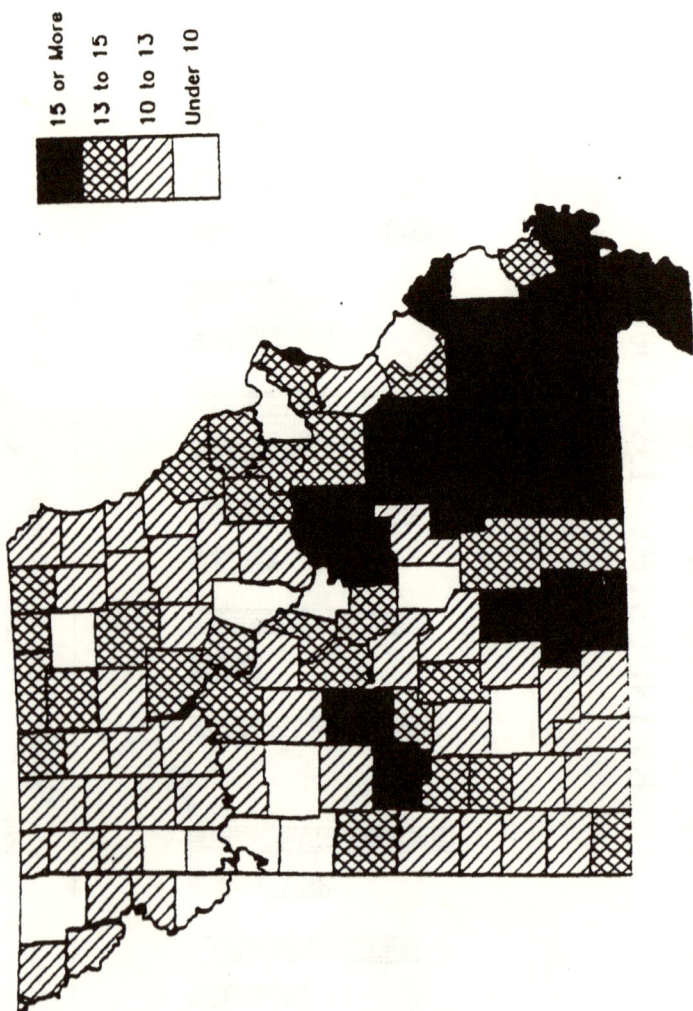

Legend:
- 15 or More
- 13 to 15
- 10 to 13
- Under 10

10

The Graduate Curriculum:
Notes on What's Right / Wrong with It

GERALD GILLESPIE
Stanford University

I am commenting personally as a comparatist one of whose major subfields is German literature and culture; I am not representing the German group or program at Stanford. Rather than spell out how I understand my work as a comparatist over the past thirty years, I refer you to my statement in the volume *Building a Profession*, edited by Spariosu and Gossman, and to my more recent articles on the global context of Comparative Literature. As relevant background for the local situations of *Germanistik* or Germanics or German Studies in the United States, I ask you to keep in mind a host of givens that various commentators here and elsewhere have noted as factors leading into our present chaotic variety of American graduate programs: for instance, the demographic, generational, and intellectual shifts in our own ranks and institutions since World War II; the persistent differences in program sizes and structures across the USA.; the implications of the unification of Europe and the disintegration of the Soviet empire; the triumph of English as the global lingua franca; and so forth.

Another natural given is that our graduate programs have always been caught in a field of forces between full-scale European departments of German and North American departments of English. American departments or sub-departments devoted to particular

overseas cultures, such as the Bengali, or Chinese, or German, have
striven to convey an enormous material within its special contexts,
but have operated with a fraction of the resources available for representing the surrounding dominant Anglo-American home culture.
What are negligible errors in the deployment of faculty energies in a
big English department can prove crippling for a small German(ic)
group. In historical terms, the sense of a coherent mission for foreign
literature studies is now merely a fading recollection in many parts
of the United States; it was grounded in humanist philological traditions and in the post-Romantic organicist and dialectical models of
cultural development shared across the Atlantic. This heritage of a
classical hermeneutics was still widely discernible in the early 1980s
at Stanford, even though our graduate program already styled itself
"German Studies" by the early 1970s. We related multi-directionally
with other programs and mounted some quite abstract courses, but
we also cultivated historical awareness in our four staple tracks: German language and linguistics, German literature, German intellectual history, and German cultural studies. The ambitious Stanford
German Studies project was conceived when the department counted
some fifteen persons in the professorate. After suffering retrench-
ment to only six persons (several being shared with other programs),
the department has to consider more soberly the probable repercussions of investing any potential resources in fragmented islets of sub-
specialization.

     As an American comparatist cross-appointed in German Studies,
I am concerned about the widespread failure in the United States to
make a positive transition to a more complicated sense of mission,
but this conference at Vanderbilt is a heartening sign of a will to face
the challenge. Ill-thought expansionism in foreign language and literature departments under Title VII and after Sputnik has had its more
recent, often more disorderly, analogue in the stampede to accommodate comparative and interdisciplinary studies without acceptance of
the qualitative requirements for such a step. A fellow Germanist-
comparatist, Ingeborg Hoesterey, has trenchantly described the latter
malady. Too many German programs have collaborated in the neglect
of the larger repertory of European studies by allowing perhaps ir-
reparable ruptures in their own core curricula—a syndrome of the

non-replacement of expertise in too many crucial sectors, too swiftly. Being closer in bulk to English departments, some larger German departments, such as at the big Midwestern schools and the University of Washington, may have the manoeuvre room to maintain sufficient vital points of reference while experimenting. But smaller German departments, including those at prestigious schools which pride themselves on being lean and mean, court real dangers when they try to become followers of glamorous trends in a time of contraction. The great state universities may indeed play an increasingly important part in rescuing Germanics and German Studies by cultivating something that more closely resembles the shape of a rich, fuller program.

As said, the standard of comparison across the nation will remain America's great English departments, which have their Alfred, Chaucer, Shakespeare, Milton, and other lights down to the present, as well as the imposing list of major thinkers and doers on this side of the water in the Anglo-American stream. In my view, German graduate programs in the United States reduce their chances of looking and being strong if they strip away scarce anchor points of program content, because these bestow longer-term credibility and recognizability. Some smaller outfits may wisely consolidate by combining one or two generalists with one or two specialists in core subject-matters. By providing a friendly home for some experts who cultivate awareness of great authors or periods, German programs maintain program identity and an awareness of the reality of scholarly depth in the field.

When condemnation of 'Eurocentrism' dissipates, as it will (even in key English departments still lost in that haze), many a small German program in America will find it has been suckered into a game sponsored mainly by local nativist lobbies. In the long haul, it will be the clever Americanists who win out in America in the process of fragmenting other people's disciplines into redistributive fiefdoms beholden to their Americanist themes, just as in France it will be the specialists in French culture and its sociolects who carry the day.

Investigating the role of Italian migrants in Argentina or the influence of German slang in elitist schools in Japan is certainly worthwhile, but if such activities permanently replace searching attention to significant works by writers of Italian and German expression in European culture, American administrators will question whether Italian or German programs have any serious distinct object of study, and whether most of their respective curricula should be reassigned to the social science departments. Teaching topics in German for the laudable sake of conveying advanced vocabulary to non-native speakers will not offer an adequate disguise for a weak or self-destructive curriculum. I leave it to you to fill in mentally your own list of those colleagues in German graduate programs who, using their own favorite meta-narrative, exert themselves to demonstrate to their university communities that German literature, or indeed all literature, is disreputable or irrelevant, if not effectively dead. This message, too, in either German or English, is one of a set of propositions that handily identify a unit which a responsible administrator can scrap without loss.

I can assure you that my national and international work as an editor in a number of capacities involves me regularly in considering a wide variety of philosophical, sociological, anthropological, and psychological approaches. Far from rejecting the value of findings based on the "human sciences," I believe that, as academic citizens, comparatists who contribute to the affairs of foreign language and literature groups have a special obligation to marshall the data in a constructive way. Anyone who analyzes relationships among language and literature departments in India, Ireland, or Italy can extrapolate lessons applicable in America to the specific conditions of America.

One of the most important is that our German graduate curricula should posit at most only a few distinct, attainable areas of study. A second is that these in the aggregate must reflect an intellectual integrity high enough to offset the natural constant doubt about the cost of representing insights about and from overseas cultures rather than devoting and diverting even more energy and resources to the materials of the native tradition. In America as in Brazil, the native tradition includes the melange of items loosely termed "multiculturalism."

Several colleagues have spoken earlier about the misalignments and displacements in the graduate training of Germanists—about how, for example, our undergraduates often encounter green TAs, not seasoned regular faculty, and so forth. I want to look at another part of the picture—the preparation of Ph.D. candidates in literary and cultural studies. I teach both intellectual history and literary theory, as well as literature. It is my view that neither theory nor charisma can replace cultural knowledge; and the literature is the main repository thereof. In a highly foreshortened fashion, I shall sketch advisable moves to foster cultural knowledge at the graduate level, under two categories: staffing and curricular development. The key, as ever, is a balance between excellence and coverage.

Under category one (staffing), I believe that all literature departments or sections must examine rigorously any appeal to hire a person who is recommended as being "interdisciplinary." Will the appointment truly add or replace qualitative and quantitative program elements, or will it effectively subtract from and displace the identity of the field, as has occurred in several departments at my own university, with negative consequences?

Under both categories (staffing and curriculum), I believe foreign literature departments will benefit if they emphasize broad cultural knowledge and reasoned critical approaches over "performative" representation of cultural attitudes or ideologies. That is, departments waste positions by hiring fetishistic adherents and activists instead of experts.

Under category two (curriculum), I think it is essential to assert the continuing role of Europe as a fountainhead of values and patterns in the contemporary world and the creative role of the territories within this major ancestral civilization from which that of the Americas springs. Space forbids laying out the historical evidence for this view, but it is the kind of substantive matter a curriculum can and ought to develop.

In rethinking its curriculum, a German department or section can profitably consider supporting the creation of a substantive European studies program or more specifically a German area program. Examples would be West European Studies at Indiana and the Institute for German Studies at Cornell. This sort of tie is preferable to being amalgamated in an ill-defined jumble of language and literature units, where everything field-specific can become hostage to the lowest common denominator and nativist lobbies can seek to enforce subservience to their goals.

I have not yet touched on the thorny decision which some administrators will try to push through: the separation of all foreign
language training into a separate pedagogical unit, and the amalgama-
tion of all foreign literary and cultural studies in another unit, often
under the aegis of supposedly superior types like 'comparatists' or
'theorists.'

In my view, comparatists and devotees of theory possess no special competence to determine the welfare of the whole complex of
traditional departments or sections. It is no secret that comparatists
and theory advocates, too, can become imperialist wreckers instead
of allies. (The majority of all the foreign language and literature
groups, including the comparatists, I am happy to note, have fero-
ciously opposed this sort of over-simplifying plan recently at Stanford. There was a general realization that external agendas were
driving the process—not the view of their mission held by the actual
experts. It remains to be seen whether the faculty's will can prevail.)

I do not believe there is a hard and fast rule that governs this
issue. But it is vital that German departments or sections carefully
consider the pragmatic repercussions a reorganization may have on
graduate training. Will it be possible to mount elegant courses and
seminars using linguistically difficult texts in an environment designed for generalists, and perhaps swarming with poorly informed
anti-European instructors? I do not say this in a partisan spirit because I feel threatened personally as a Germanist; rather, as a comparatist with proven interests in Western European and New World
literatures and in the variegated literary realities of other continents,
I sense that, objectively, it is my "type" of scholar who poses a gen-
uine threat to many deserving Germanists under the current dispen-
sation at many American universities.

These, to sum up briefly, are some of the strengths which exist in
many current German graduate programs and ought to be further cultivated or introduced upon opportunity:

• Most advanced programs should concentrate on literature as
their main sphere. Few possess a critical mass of competence in another sphere.

- Even hard-strapped programs should stretch themselves to include training in German literature and cultural history of the medieval and early modern periods.

- Programs should include courses that reach across to other media—for example, opera, film, painting, etc.

- To the extent feasible, programs should invite German writers and artists for brief visits or a residency.

- Programs should promote regular exchange of their students to European universities as part of degree preparation.

- Programs should never relegate students or teachers to lower status because they opt to specialize intensively in Germanics. Generalist and comparative studies are not more virtuous; they are only of a different order.

- By the same token, graduate programs should accommodate double degrees, combining Germanics with (an)other advanced field(s), and should make generalists and comparatists genuinely welcome. Ordinarily this cannot occur unless some substantial number of the advanced courses are conducted in English, at least alternately with German in the case of perennial offerings.

- To this extent, the "Americanization" of the curriculum is today a social and intellectual necessity. Such high level cross-fertilization will benefit the entire institutional curricular range.

The field of Germanics faces a double bind at the end of this century. On the one hand, it will fade out of the American picture of the humanities if Germanists do not actively make and use translations and teach the significant German works also in English at all curricular levels. On the other hand, it will disappear by cooptation if it fails to maintain a distinct profile separate from generalist and comparative studies and fails to prepare specialists with deep expertise.

Works Cited

Gillespie, Gerald. "Home Truths & Institutional Falsehoods." In: *Building a Profession: Autobiographical Perspectives on the Beginnings of Comparative Literature in the United States.* Ed. by Lionel Gossman and Mihai I, Spariosu. Albany: State University of New York Press, 1994. 159-175.

———. "Rhinoceros, Unicorn, or Chimera?—A Polysystemic View of Possible Kinds of Comparative Literature in the New Century." *Journal of Intercultural Studies* 19 (1992): 14-21.

———. "Comparative Literature of the 1990s in the USA" In: *Issues and Methods in Comparative Studies.* Ed. by Tania Franco Carvalhal. (forthcoming)

Hoesterey, Ingeborg. "Culture Studies and Its Discontents." Paper presented at the German Studies Association conference in Dallas, 1994. [I am grateful to Prof. Hoesterey for supplying me with a copy of her ms.]

11

On the Graduate Curriculum:
What's Right / Wrong With It?

JANE K. BROWN
University of Washington

The nature of a specifically American graduate program that prepares its students to teach in American institutions of higher education is determined, of course, by one's vision of the American undergraduate program. My starting point is that all the courses of the latter, whether major courses, courses in translation, or language courses, should contribute to the basic goals of an American college education: namely, the development of critical thinking, reading, and writing. That being said, I would like to take a pragmatic and empirical approach to the graduate program in a specifically "American" German department by discussing the subtext of our graduate program, which we reorganized a few years ago. A lot of time and energy goes into revising curricula, and I think it is generally time well spent. Nevertheless, we should not lose sight of the fact that the curriculum and requirements are really only a part of a graduate program, and perhaps not in the long run the most influential part. Ultimately the coherence of the curriculum derives less from its structure, often difficult to implement as planned in a small program, than from the ethos of the department, the shared values of the faculty. This ethos comes into play most effectively during hiring and graduate admissions. I am going to offer you an idealized description of our department ethos in terms of six categories, with some description to make clear what I mean.

First, my colleagues tend to agree that knowledge in our discipline is best organized in historical terms, hence our curriculum is
basically organized in terms of periods. Although we do not have the
resources to offer full coverage of all historical areas of the curriculum (we can field only 8 or 9 graduate seminars per year, or about
three per quarter) we do have at least one person prepared and willing
to teach each area. But we also believe that providing an historical
scope is an individual as well as a departmental function. We are
training our students to teach, frequently, in very small departments
where they will of necessity be generalists. Thus we consider it important to set an example to students by offering both historical
range and flexibility.

Second, we tend to agree on the need for similar flexibility and
breadth toward the skills of the discipline. What German culture has
to offer the American curriculum is not just a collection of good
books but a capacity to abstract and theorize—an interest in ideas,
the German tradition of idealism—that is not indigenous to the more
pragmatic Anglo-American tradition and certainly not readily found
in the graduate of the average American high school. This capacity
has surely been the great legacy of the distinguished German philo-
sophic tradition, to which Germanistik as practiced in Germany as
well as in the U.S. has been perhaps not as open as it ought to be. Indeed, Gadamer, Heidegger, Nietzsche, Freud, Marx often have more
play in French and English departments than in German. How is it
that the German scholars who have had more influence on how people in this country read—Auerbach, Spitzer, Curtius, perhaps also
Jauß and Iser—were (apart from the Anglist Iser) Romanists? How is
it that the author of the new Duden Grammatik der deutschen
Sprache, Harald Weinrich, is a Romanist? As my examples, and indeed, my department shows, I do not mean that we should all be
teaching theory. Far from it. But it is crucial that our graduate training at least encourage students to engage critically with their own activity as readers and scholars and to be aware of alternatives
articulated outside of Germanics.

Third, to balance the flexibility, it is important to us that we pre-
serve coherence despite the variety of approaches represented among

the faculty. Thus while the specific interests of members of our faculty range between the extremes of historical philology and linguistics, on the other hand, and cultural criticism on the other, they are held together by a common commitment to a middle ground of hermeneutics. I think we all regard our discipline as an interpretive one, and our main teaching function as training students to interpret, to read and write thoughtfully and critically. This central commitment is what we hold in common with most English departments; it is, ultimately, what justifies our presence on an undergraduate campus. When we hire we attend closely to the quality of the reading and writing of our candidates, and we screen applicants to the graduate program primarily on the basis of writing samples. That is why undergraduate English majors sometimes are seen as stronger applicants to our program than many German majors.

Fourth, our primary concern with training in analysis and writing is met by having all the courses be seminars in which the students are expected to write seminar papers. (The only exception are the linguistics courses, the required introduction to teaching language, and the strongly recommended introduction to bibliography/critical approaches.) Seminar topics are chosen by the individual faculty members, a built-in assurance of methodological breadth. Simple guidelines maintain historical scope in the overall pattern of offerings. Although we do not expect all of our graduate students to teach in research universities and be publishing scholars, we do believe that all good teachers continue to learn and to develop their own ideas, and that the best training for a career of continued growth is to try out the scholarly practice offered in research seminars. (We did not set out to reinvent the wheel.) We talked about designing a required introductory seminar in writing, but could not agree on a model that more than a single member of the faculty was committed to; it did not seem wise to institute a requirement on such a narrow base. The effect of the discussion, nevertheless, was to raise the consciousness of all of us that teaching writing was an integral component of all our courses.

How each of us goes about the task is a touchy thing to regulate, so it remains highly individual. In my own teaching and advising I focus a lot on basic writing strategies at the level of paragraphing, the function and structure of introductions and conclusions, and the like. I also try to get students to think about the cultural differences in academic writing—the different scope and function of introductions in German essays, the location of ideas at the beginnings rather than at the ends of paragraphs. Finally, I try to get them to think about the particular audience they want to address in their scholarly work, and about the relationship of that audience to their teaching audience.

Fifth, there is what I would like to think of as the cosmopolitanism of our department, what we have been talking about here as visibility. The interpretive skills we teach can be brought to bear on phenomena besides German texts: texts in other languages, art, music, social structures. Hence our openness to other areas, including other literatures, other arts, cultural studies, European area studies. In fact, the University of Washington has just set up a West European Studies Center and an undergraduate program in European Studies; we have been involved in these efforts since their early planning stages. This is not a matter of our going out and becoming historians or political scientists or anthropologists. It is rather a matter of carrying our own materials into a different forum, and sometimes of bringing our particular philological and hermeneutic skills to bear on materials other than literature.

Recently, I was approached by a professor of Forestry desperate for assistance in presenting Faust responsibly to his students, whom he thinks need exposure to the ethical issues raised by the text. It was a new idea to me that we had a responsibility to bring our relevant texts to his attention (not wait for him to find them in an airport, as in this case, but I think he is right. We in our department do some teaching in our university's evening degree program—not very successfully (i.e. we don't attract many students)—but nothing for students in professional programs. And we have not begun to think about how to prepare our graduate students to teach these mature students with no background in literature. Currently we allocate one third of our courses to the undergraduate program (including non-major courses in English), and one third to the graduate program. I no longer think the balance is correct; more resources should be built into non-major courses, whether as our own or courses contributed to other programs.

It also worries me that our hiring process tends to favor candidates with more training in comparative literature than we encourage for our own graduate students. It takes a certain cosmopolitanism to be interested in things German—we had better be leading examples of cosmopolitanism in our college communities.

Finally, there is language teaching and training in teaching. Our ethos is that they are important. So the language coordinator is hired with great care, holds a regular line appointment, teaches literature and culture, was actively supported by all colleagues for the university teaching award. Regular faculty teaching at any level of the language program work under his supervision—happily I should add. In addition to this example, graduate students get a lot of guidance and pressure to work and consult together about teaching. Much of what they learn about language teaching is transferable to literature teaching; we encourage the connection by giving advanced graduate students opportunity to assist in undergraduate literature courses—and by setting the example of a department in which all the regular faculty teach at all levels.

Personally, I think we should be cultivating a more intimate relation between language teaching and literature teaching by changing the focus of the language program away from communication and toward literacy. Good critical skills depend on sensitivity to language and the ways it is used. Good language teaching should cultivate this sensitivity at every turn. It should itself contribute to training students to be critical in their use of language, whether or not they will ever use the target language. To my mind this it the most legitimate justification of foreign-language requirements. The opacity of a foreign language actually makes the task of teaching students to think about language as a phenomenon much easier than when students are introduced to interpretation in English, for the need to deal with the particularities of language is much less obvious in one's native language. This means, of course, focusing on the particularities of language (semantics and syntax), on strategies for dealing with the limitations of one's control, paying more attention to the written language and the relation of language to literacy than to the rough and ready communication in daily situations that is now in style.

The various aspects of the ethos I have described engage the dif-

ferent aspects that have accrued to literary study since its first documented appearance in fifth-century Greece. There Homer's Iliad was
used to train children in ethics, the demand still being placed on us
by our non-majors—my forester for example. Training in writing has
become gradually and increasingly our purview since literature became entangled with rhetoric in late antiquity. Since the Renaissance
philology, translation, and language training have been central com-
ponents, and in the course of the eighteenth century philology expanded to embrace the history first of language, then of literature and
culture, then of ideas, and most recently of thought. Finally, beginning in the romantic period, reflection on the act of reading,
hermeneutics—now full-blown into theory—joined the roster. On-
togeny recapitulates phylogeny, biologists tell us. That is why we
need to have room for all these categories in our graduate teaching.

12

The Americanization of German Studies: The Curriculum

KEITH BULLIVANT
UNIVERSITY OF FLORIDA

There is, of course, something truly grotesque about a recently arrived Brit of all people standing here today and talking about the Americanization of our subject. I can only hope that, not having grown up in this particular academic environment, but rather having come late to it, my observations about the curriculum here and my comparisons with the situation in Great Britain will shed a different light on the state of our discipline.

When I arrived here in January 1989 I discovered that, despite my previous visits and what I thought was careful research, I was not prepared for the reality of everyday life in a German department. Two things in particular stood out: the dominance of native-born Germans on many faculties, ones different from those that had excited me at conferences or through their publications, and the old-fashionedness—to my way of thinking—of many curricula.

Let me step back a little now and put all this into the context of my socialization. For reasons that have to do with England's not being, historically, a country of immigrants, but above all because of the origins, course and consequences of the two World Wars, the German Germanist was until relatively recently a rarity in Britain and the profession continues to be dominated by the British. From this developed a clear sense of purpose. If we look at the work of the generation of Roy Pascal and Richard Hinton Thomas then it is evident that they saw their most important task as mediating German culture to a British audience: they wrote in English for that audience, translated or encouraged the translation of key German texts and wrote many an introduction to the standard translations that could be found on the shelves of city libraries. Until well into the sixties, however, the canon that they propagated—again for reasons that have to do with Germany's role in world history in the first half of this century—was an understandably sanitized and reassuring one that they shared with Emil Staiger, with virtually the whole of West German Germanistik and, so I learn from Hinrich Seeba, also their American counterparts. This same sort of canon, still in surprisingly rude health, was to confront me again when I moved to the States. In the course of the sixties, however, things began to change. As early as 1963 Richard Hinton Thomas was appointed Professor of Modern German Studies at Birmingham University and a program of systematic syllabus reform begun at both undergraduate and graduate level; the influence of Raymond Williams, Richard Hoggart and Stuart Hall cannot be understated here, either. Courses in German philosophy and sociology were introduced, the Frankfurt School discovered, the syllabi extended to take in National Socialism, the culture of the Weimar Republic, Naturalism, the Vormärz, and film, for example. Instead of the language being taught as a "zweites Latein" emphasis was now placed increasingly on oral and written competence in the living language; very quickly a compulsory year of study in West Germany was demanded of undergraduates. Reform of the graduate curriculum quickly followed.

Looking back, it becomes clear that—notwithstanding the pioneering role of people like Pascal and Hinton Thomas—the ultimately successful struggle to establish a new understanding of our discipline was very much a generational one—with a key role being played by a younger generation of Germanisten with a different attitude towards Germany and the Germans from their predecessors. But it was more than a generational struggle: it was also an anti-establishment one, with new programs challenging the negative weight of tradition represented by the older ones, with Oxford and Cambridge being here especially important. But during the course of the eighties the battle was definitively won, as a generational change came about and programs came under the guidance of professors influenced both by a new generation of Germanisten in West Germany and also by the work of American ones like Frank Trommler and Jost Hermand, whose work had long been recognized as embodying the necessary focus of German Studies.

As in the US, the experience of the Student Revolt of 1968 and its impact on conventional wisdoms about university studies, were of particular significance in the UK. Crucial too was the support offered at this time by the DAAD and the Goethe Institute to new initiatives. There are, inevitably, still conservative enclaves and the occasional resistant colleague, but the bulk of programs in the UK are no longer language and literature ones, but German Studies ones. Moreover, such programs are increasingly being offered in combination with another, more practical discipline, with the aim of improving the employability of students, or as part of a multi-disciplinary package. Recent statistics in an article in the DAAD's *Info DaF* indicate that only 29% of British undergraduates study Germanistik as a major and, with the exception of Oxford, Cambridge and University College, London, most graduate programs consequently look something like that of the Center for German and European Studies at Georgetown. The M.A. is now regarded in the main as a terminal degree leading somewhere outside the academy, rather than as a stepping-stone to a Ph.D. program.

This then was my background before I came to the States. I spoke earlier of a sense of shock when I arrived, and I'll come back to that. But I should say that my perhaps naive expectations as far as a discourse with colleagues old and new were concerned have not been disappointed and I am grateful for the way in which the profession has embraced me here. I continue to be impressed by the quality and theoretical bite of the *research* of colleagues, and particularly of younger colleagues, here in the States. But back to the sense of shock. One reason why I came to the States was because of the way colleagues I had met at conferences in Europe stimulated me; over and above that a range of important books and the work published in journals such as *German Studies Review, New German Critique* and *The German Quarterly* led me to believe that German Studies in the

US were much further advanced than was even the case in England.

What I was not aware of was the sheer number of German native speakers here—not the ones whose work I knew, but German exiles living in a sort of time and language warp, i.e. not linguistically or culturally integrated here and leading in their teaching and research the life of a Germanist of yesteryear, with the focus always on the debate with often erudite areas of German Germanistik and with publication exclusively in the appropriate German periodical. I'm not saying that participation in that debate or publication in Germany is wrong, indeed, as someone more than once accused by his British colleagues of being obsessed with these I am the last person who could or would say that. However, I believe it crucial that we "Auslandsgermanisten" not only maintain that discourse with Germany, but also continue in our mission of mediating German culture to our American public, in the first instance our students.

Although Valters Nollendorfs has shown that their presence is diminishing and will continue to do so, the dominance of this 'time-warp' generation and also those American pupils under its influence is very real, in my experience. It is manifested above all, I would argue, in our syllabi, important changes in which are also the subject of our next session. Despite the quality of much individual research and the intellectual stimulus of, for example, the special number of *The German Quarterly* on German Studies that greeted me when I arrived in the Spring of 1989, I find myself having to agree to some extent with Peter Uwe Hohendahl, who argued in that edition that "the majority of German departments in the country have continued to define their programs in terms of the accepted literary canon, adding civilization and film courses on the margin to make the program more appealing to a new generation of students." I think though it should be said, to be fair, that many departments have gone further, adding new courses on theory, on women's writing and on exile literature, work in this area is one of the special achievements of American Germanistik.

However, if we look at the course requirements for M.A. programs, we see that Hohendahl is essentially correct: the major emphasis of curricula is still on the traditional core of our discipline and many of the M.A. reading lists I have seen in the States still reflect the canon of the fifties, as required by the would-be 'Studienrat' of the day, now augmented by the tokenist addition of some female names, which in turn necessitate a thinning out of the earlier canon. Advanced undergraduate courses in which we prepare our majors for commencing graduate work are, inevitably, pale reflections of these, with surveys of the major literary periods, movements and genres holding center stage. Our training consequently prepares good students to go on to graduate work, to qualify via the Master's program for the Ph.D. program and in time to become university teachers of the same sort of German course. It does not, however, offer them a Master's that prepares them to become high-school teachers of German in the American system, nor does it give them the sort of awareness of German culture in its societal context that could help them in other later employment situations.

Change of, or at the very least, alternatives to, our existing German courses at the undergraduate and graduate level are necessary if German Studies are to appear to future American students to be a relevant discipline offering a number of realistic career paths and if German Studies are to meet some of the needs of this country in the international market place of the twenty-first century. To make such changes is not easy and is much more difficult here than it was in Britain, where a norm of eight years of high-school German and a more concentrated period of undergraduate study give the average beginning graduate student a breadth and depth of coverage just not attainable here at that level. The preconditions for a redefinition of the subject were so much more favorable, but nevertheless, even there the wider focus of German Studies demanded a willingness to break with received wisdom as to the core of our subject. Perhaps the most extreme example is the newly founded—with money from the DAAD—Institute for German Studies at the University of Birmingham, where the emphasis, at least initially, is exclusively on the social sciences.

Without necessarily following that particular course, radical thinking will be all the more necessary here, given the short time-span of the average American's study of German. Can we expect graduate students to continue to study the History of the Language, Medieval Literature, the Baroque and all the other component parts of the canon and at the same time cope with the demands of an intensive and extensively demanding new discourse focussed on the modern and contemporary, now even more necessary than ever after German unification? Certainly not at the M.A. level I would argue, where change needs to start, particularly if this is again to be conceived as a worthwhile terminal degree in itself. But if we do try to change things, our discipline will have to contend with the conservative, normative pressure exerted by the tradition of Germanistik in this country, a tradition centered on the canon. This has led so many departments to fall between stools: the canon, by now more a daisy, in Valters Nollendorfs' loving image, for me more of a "Rumpfkanon," is not taught with the rigor and extensiveness of yore. But no breakthrough to a new coherent discourse is made.

Two ways out of the impasse suggest themselves here, based on my observations of developments in Great Britain. One, certainly the most radical and certain to be challenged by the weight of tradition, would be for some departments to go the extra step and define the focus of our subject as *Modern* German Studies in the sense of a delimiting of the period of study to, for example, 1750 up to the present, which would make room for the extensiveness needed to examine the range of German culture in the period adequately. The second set of possibilities might, for example, designate such an approach as forming the core of the undergraduate curriculum and then allow for various paths through the graduate degree—a linguistic one, a more historical or a more literary one, but also one that allowed for a deepening and widening of the path of Modern German Studies begun at the major level. This is an approach that would seem to be being developed in a number of graduate programs—Georgetown obviously comes to mind here—in the last few years. And such a more pluralist compromise at least has the potential to address to some extent the biggest obstacle to a thoroughgoing modernisation of our discipline: we, the faculty.

13

Disciplining Boundaries

WOLFGANG NATTER
University of Kentucky

For those of us who approach this *fin de siècle* as teachers and scholars housed in U.S. departments of Germanistics, "Foreign" Languages, and German Studies, the question of where to locate the disciplinary *Standort* of our inquiry is not self-evident. The question equally invites consideration of both disciplines and identities as forcefull categories as well as that of boundaries—as in how and why limits are or become fixed.[1] Each of these related issues may be thought of as occupying or constituting space as well as subjects and objects. In what follows, I argue on behalf of a notion of disciplines and identities which are porous, performative and non-essential. The productive force of the boundary—usually thought of as a limit, margin or border, here becomes the place where difference becomes visible through identity's dislocation. At the boundary, there becomes

[1] The present essay was originally presented to the 1994 German Studies Association annual meeting as part of a session on "German Studies/Cultural Studies and the Question of Disciplines." My thanks to the other presenters and participants on the panel, Ingeborg Hoesterey, Maximilian Aue, Paul Michael Lützeler, and Gisela Brinker-Gabler. Additional special thanks are due John McCarthy and Richard Zipser for their impressive organization of the conference on the future prospects of *Germanistik*; I am grateful for the inclusion of my essay in this volume.

visible what in fact seems always operative: identity is constituted by exclusion. Individual, national, and disciplinary identity depends upon a series of others "without" and "within." As regards "Germany," the non-essential selves which constitute an imaginary German self have been Jews, Vaterlandlose Gesellen—women and men—other Europeans and non-Europeans towards the east and west, north and south. The title of this thought-piece, "disciplining boundaries," thus refers us to the process of identity formation which institutes boundaries via exclusion and yet qua excluded allows the identities thereby structured to set themselves apart.

This process and the identifications it engenders, works at many scales, from the individual to the regional as well as at educational levels where lines of demarcation are institutionally territorialized. If we think of "Germany" less as a ground or *Grund* than as an "Abgrund," (following a thought Thomas Mann expressed in his essay "Von Deutscher Republik" but which of course has a long history of precursors) we then approach "Germany" as a performative ideal, a place which is not surfeited by reference to the territory which that nation happens to occupy at any given time nor to the hegemony of a particular social formation in that space/time. As Hinrich Seeba suggested some years ago in an important issue of *The German Quarterly*: "German identity can only be a fiction in a no-man's land," alternatively, a 'utopian' site of fiction," or once again, an ideal, an expectation, a project that is present only in its fictional representation.[2] I don't see what would have changed since 1989 in this regard. The identity of disciplines that study Germany, the disciplinary practices which sustain them, and the range of objects of inquiry embraced by these, likewise can be understood as plural nodal points of identification, temporary fixations always potentially subject to contestation and reformulation—though usually at the boundaries.

Regions or nations are many things to many people over time, but as bounded entities, self-contained and subject to independent laws they are principly heuristic devices, frames that provide a scale

---

[2] Hinrich Seeba, "Critique of Identity Formation: Toward an Intercultural Model of German Studies," *The German Quarterly* 61 (1989): 144-54; here 149.

through which particulars and the general may be approached. Germany as the ground of German studies is a region through which the global may be examined in all its local complexity, a nexus of multiple and overdetermined points of identification with historical and spatial specificity. As such, Germany is not "natural," despite the efforts of much post-enlightenment scholarship to ground its identity there. As Jeff Peck has commented, "The history of Germanistik provides convincing evidence for the way a sphere of knowledge has been territorialized intellectually and geographically, since these histories have attempted to construct a certain coherent notion of 'German' grounded in a specific place."[3] German identity—in the singular—proves to be a performative principle, which two centuries of Germanistik (and other disciplinary practices) did everything to make concrete or give the appearance of the necessary. If by contrast, "german" identity returns toward the formulation where it usually has been—towards questions of "German identities"—then, a way of apprehending the contingent though interested, provisional though monumentally framed character of disciplinary self-definitions, norms and practices likewise come into view. A number of the social sciences and humanities have in fact become more open to recognizing the non-monumental character of their articulated histories. For those of us housed in German departments there is no shortage of historical reasons why this should be so.

If we can denaturalize the disciplinary histories of Germanistik, history, geography or sociology (for example), it is because each would clearly seem to be a discipline. What about German Studies? Is it a discipline? A field, or area of concentration? How is a discipline different from a *Fach* or *Gebiet*? *Gebiet* suggests a linkage between the frames of geographic and academic location and hence useful here. The term also suggests something both specific and open, like the territorial region, a heuristic device, a provisional identity, open at the boundaries. Heidrun Suhr has recently summarized German studies in this way: "German Studies is a critique of the dis-

---

[3] Jeff Peck, "There's No Place Like Home? Remapping the Topography of German Studies," *The German Quarterly* 62.2 (1989): 178-87; here 180.

ciplinary way Germanistik, German history, German politics were
taught and researched and as an active critique, German studies can
focus on questions of the boundaries of the discipline, the exclusion
of the so-called marginal issues and be self reflective to its own development in the emerging field."[4] Importantly, she notes that "the
term German Studies defies simple definition. It has been applied in
a number, sometimes even contradictory, ways, it is amorphous and
inconclusive in itself, but offers multiple possibilities to exploit this
very fact on practical and theoretical levels" (Suhr 115). Like most of
the contributors to the above mentioned 1989 special issue of *German Quarterly*, Suhr's vision of German Studies suggests a *Gebiet*
whose intellectual vitality is premised upon its resistance to self-en-
closure, and in that I see a chance for our field that is linked to another as equally porous and open, namely cultural studies. The 1992
volume of essays assembled under the title *Cultural Studies* not only
documents how difficult it is to define "it" just now, but Angela
McRobbie, looking ahead to the future of these studies, affirms that
"[F]or cultural studies to survive it cannot afford to lose this disciplinary looseness, this feeling that, like other radical areas of inquiry,
such as psychoanalysis, its authors are making it up as they go
along."[5]

One of the major theoretical advancements of cultural studies
was the dismantling of the Marxist base/superstructure paradigm,
whose result has been to locate culture rather than the economy as
the primary site of *political* struggle. But just as some vulgar Marx-
ists prioritize to a fault the role of the economic base in determining
power relations, some cultural work seems to overemphasize culture's role in maintaining dominance or, more commonly, providing
opportunities for resistance. Clearly, such an impulse is tied to the

---

[4] Heidrun Suhr, "German Studies in North America: Contexts and Perspectives,"
in *Präludien. Kanadisch-Deutsche Dialoge*, ed. Burkhard Krause, Ulrich Scheck, and
Patrick O'Neill (München: Judicium Verlag, 1992), 105-119; here 116.
[5] Angele McRobbie, "Post-Marxism and Cultural Studies: A Post-Script," in *Cultural Studies*, ed. by Lawrence Grossberg, Cary Nelson, and Paula Treichler (New
York: Routledge, 1992), 719-30; here 722.

attempt to link a field to the lived experience of people in contemporary society, and, "from the bottom up" in a manner that rejects the stupification thesis so central to an avant-guard conception of culture. It seems to me that quite a bit of extremely valuable research needs to be done in examining the lived experiences of various generations within our *Gebiet*. I would caution, however, that we will not want to forget "high culture" or the sphere of so called autonomous art in the process. Adorno's critique of Benjamin's *Kunstwerk* essay seems relevant here at least to the extent that viewing "popular" culture dialectically and in intertextual relation to other social products should not foreclose the gains to be expected from doing the same with "autonomous art."[6] As German Studies continues to move beyond the relatively closed world of literary works and their institutional horizons of reception, we also should not loose sight of the fact that "replacing literature with culture (in the anthropological sense) as the field of research and teaching also significantly broadens the theoretical horizon."[7] Quite a bit of theoretical work will accompany any sustained fusing of horizons of signification between Germanistics and those fields which can contribute to the present tasks because of differing methods, aims and objects inscribed in their various disciplinary histories.

An understanding of the text as a social product, which takes into account both its use value and its production as a social process, invites the kind of thinking in which other disciplines can join us. Texts (as well as "works"), understood as social products, exist materially. A text must be written, printed, or electronically displayed for it to enter social life. Books, for example, have a substance and materiality without which their message cannot enter circulation. Writers and their intentions form only one part of this social process. It is es-

---

[6] In this regard see Adorno's letters to Benjamin: Walter Benjamin, "Zeugnisse zur Entstehungsgeschichte," *Gesammelte Schriften*, ed. by Rolf Tiedemann and Hermann Schweppenhauser, vol. V-2: *Das Passagen-Werk* (Frankfurt a.M.: Suhrkamp, 1972), 1081-1206.

[7] Peter U. Hohendahl, "Interdisciplinary German Studies: Tentative Conclusions," *The German Quarterly* 62.2 (1989): 227-34; here 233.

sential to remember that no text exists outside of the support that enables it to be read; any comprehension of a writing, no matter what it is, depends upon the forms in which it reaches its reader. Implicated in this understanding of literature as a social process are publishing houses, booksellers, the academy, and the state, all of which promote and inhibit the parameters of the iterable in any given space and time.

For many colleagues of my generation housed in German departments, German studies *has been* cultural studies—a *Gebiet* at the boundary of literary studies which has given productive reasons as to why we should extend the list of questions we ask of our inherited objects of inquiry to include consideration of equally pertinent cultural, social, political contexts while at the same time extending such text-context analysis outside the confines of the traditional canon. Such an understanding, I believe, would link the productive theoretical impulses in cultural studies—considerations regarding identity and identification—to the German Studies model envisioned by so many of us here.

Let me spell out some of the reasons why in my remaining time by reference again to disciplines, identities, and the question of boundaries. I do so by allusion to some recent thought of Chantal Mouffe, a political philosopher, who has formulated some implications which derive from a poststructural notion of the constitutive outside. In her own work and in collaboration with Ernesto LaClau, Mouffe has placed the question of identity at the core of her project of "radical and plural democracy." She stresses that every identity is relational and that the condition of existence of every identity is the affirmation of a difference, the determination of an 'other' that will play the role of a 'constitutive outside." Thus, following the notion of the 'constitutive outside', the outside is actively present 'inside,' and it is always a real possibility that arrangements will be re-negotiated:

> Once it is acknowledged that any identity is relational and defined in terms of difference, how can we defuse the possibility of exclusion that it entails? By stressing the fact that the outside is constitutive, it reveals the impossibility of drawing an absolute

distinction between interior and exterior. The existence of the other becomes the condition of possibility of my identity since without the other, I could not have an identity. Therefore every identity is irremediably destabilized by its exterior and the interior appears as something always contingent.[8]

This formulation questions every essentialist conception of identity and forecloses every attempt to define identity conclusively. Identity cannot, therefore, belong to one person alone and no-one belongs to a single identity. Mouffe goes further in arguing that "not only there are no 'natural' and 'original' identities, since every identity is the result of a constituting process, but that this process itself must be seen as one of permanent hybridization and nomadisation." As academics housed in US German departments, we belong to several communities simultaneously, each embedded in geographic, historical, and disciplinary traditions. Our identity is, in effect, the result of a multitude of interactions which take place inside a space the outlines of which are not clearly defined (Mouffe, 11).

The absence of any necessary determination of the subject in Mouffe's identity theory finds a parallel reflection at the level of collective history and tradition. Hegemonic cultural practices always attempt to fix the meaning of history and tradition, arranging any number of particularities and singular events into a manifold unity; the one story, the one identity, as in for example "nation" or other state and social formations. In the case of Germany, we need to carefully examine those historical-spatial articulations (or horizons of disarticulation in Benjamin's sense) in order to overcome the notion of a tradition which is seamless, natural, inevitable. Instead of historical and cultural markers that document a teleology of progress or its opposite, Mouffe's linkage of identity to a history of the subject's

[8] Chantal Mouffe, "Postmarxism, Democracy, and Identity," presented at the 1994 Meeting of the Association of American Geographers. The author kindly made her manuscript available to me from which I cite. The essay is to be published in revised form in the up-coming issue of *Society and Space* 13 (1995). For greater elaboration of her position see "An Interview with Chantal Mouffe," *disClosure* 3 (1993): 87-104.

identifications redirects our attention to the deployment and use value at work in forging collective identifications, understood as on-going—and contingent—historical and spatial nodal points.[9]

In the context of German studies, an engagement with cultural studies offers the promise of further examining our frame—the *Abgrund* called Germany—in all its complexity. For Germanists, this will also entail undiminished critical reflection on the overdetermined history of *Kultur* and *Kulturwissenschaften*, particularly as regards the volitions that accompanied the institutionalization of such disciplines as anthropology, geography and sociology in the 19th-century university and the social deployment of their accumulated knowledges in 20th-century German statecraft.[10] The tainted legacy of Germanistik as a "deutsche Wissenschaft" is not unique, and it warns against an uncritical adaptation of other disciplinary trajectories without similar distancing.

At least from the perspective of our own *scholarly* pursuits (separating for now the curricular aspect of discipline, i.e., how U.S. universities slot our teaching time), I find ample reasons as to why we should continue to pursue a *multidisciplinary* cultural research. I mean here to distinguish between inter- and multi-disciplinary research. As often as not, interdisciplinarity simply tends to add to the confusion. Multidisciplinary work is premised upon respect for and familiarity with the epistemologies, methodologies, and historically embedded objects of study that characterize the trajectory of any given discipline. The kind of familiarity presupposed here does not crystalize as a result of a single conference or GSA panel, but emerges only by virtue of sustained engagement and *practice*. While *Germanistik* or even German Studies is now thought of as being in a crisis of self-definition, my own multidisciplinary engagements as-

[9] Cf. also C. Mouffe and John Paul Jones, "Identity, Space, and Other Uncertainties," *Social Theory and Space: Geographical Interpretations of Postmodernism*, ed. by Georges Benko and Ulf Strohmayer (Oxford: Basil Blackwell, 1996).

[10] See Woodruff Smith, "The Emergence of the Cultural Sciences in Germany," in *Politics and the Sciences of Culture in Germany, 1840-1920* (New York: Oxford U P, 1991), who gives an account of the emergence of geography, anthropology, and sociology as a neo-liberal response to the 1848 revolution.

sure me that this 'crisis' is surely only part and parcel of a general phenomenon within the humanities and social sciences. To this phenomenon, to which I would not even want to attach the descriptor "crisis," or if so then only in the sense that organizational theory attributes to it, namely as both danger and opportunity. As Sam Weber accurately noted in 1987, this "crisis" is only

> the most obvious indication of a process of rethinking, the implications of which extend to the academic division of labor itself. As the binary, oppositional logic that has traditionally organized scientific inquiry ceases simply to be taken for granted, its institutional corollary, the procedures by which the disciplines and divisions of "scholarship" have demarcated their domains and consolidated their authority is being subjected to renewed scrutiny.[11]

Postmodernism, as an umbrella term, is also a thinking past this impasse, and as such, is tied to efforts seeking to form alternative understandings which do not rely upon the oppositional thinking which continues to organize the academy and its products. Such thinking, however, does make for an uneasy grounding of disciplinary identities, as not only their 'natural' objects of inquiry, but also their methods for rendering them, become ever less self-evident. A critical question posed under the aegis of postmodernism is how we shall react to such a scrutiny which moves past conceptions both of disciplinary boundaries as hermetically sealed, and of the entities contained within as self-referential objects subject to independent laws, principles, or rules.[12]

Against a concern that manifests itself whenever the passage

---

[11] Samuel Weber, *Institution and Interpretation* (Minneapolis: U of Minnesota P, 1987), x.

[12] Elsewhere I have argued that this self-scrutiny has implications for a number of "great divides" within the academy. See Wolfgang Natter and John Paul Jones, "Signposts Towards a Poststructural Geography," in *Postmodern Contentions: Epochs, Politics, Space*, ed. by John Paul Jones, Wolfgang Natter, and Ted Schatzki (New York: Guilford, 1993), 165-204.

from the more to the less familiar becomes evident, I would hasten
to add that it seems quite impossible to construct a "postmodern"
disciplinary practice absent of its "modern" precursors—even for
those who would wish it otherwise. Disciplines, after all, have proce-
dures through which borders are patrolled, most importantly the
principle of peer review.

I would like to close with a text rich in possibilities of what an
adequate approach to cultural studies might entail. In his inaugural
lecture held over 60 years ago, Max Horkheimer found an assessment
of the then "current crisis" that continues to resonate today:

> Although social philosophy may be at the center of the broader
> interest n philosophy, its status is no better than that of most
> contemporary philosophical or fundamental intellectual efforts.
> No substantive conceptual configuration of social philosophy
> could assert a claim to general validity. In light of the current in-
> tellectual situation, in which traditional disciplinary boundaries
> have been called into question and will remain unclear for the
> foreseeable future, it does not appear timely to attempt to delin-
> eate conclusively the various areas of research. Nonetheless, the
> general conceptions that one connects with social philosophy can
> be put concisely. Its ultimate aim is the philosophical interpreta-
> tion of the vicissitudes of human fate—the fate of humans not as
> mere individuals, however, but as members of a community. It is
> thus above all concerned with phenomena that can only be un-
> derstood in the context of human social life: with the state, law,
> economy, religion—in short, with the entire material and intel-
> lectual culture of humanity.[13]

The German cultural tradition offers ample materials—like
Horkheimer's—through which to fashion a differentiated and useable

---

[13] Max Horkheimer, "The Present Situation of Social Philosophy and the Tasks of
an Institute for Social Research," in M. H., *Between Philosophy and the Social Sciences: Selected Early Writings*, trans. by Frederick Hunter, Matthew S. Kramer, and
John Torpey (Cambridge MA: MIT Press, 1993), 1.

conceptualization of cultural studies. Our role in the current discussion regarding cultural studies might be to re-read attempts to mediate (and discipline) society, culture, and the economy, simultaneously linking and differentiating the products of this reflective enterprise to and from other traditions of cultural practice and theory.[14] This is the sense, I believe, in which German studies should become cultural studies (again).

[14] For a productive re-reading of Frankfurt-School critical theory in relationship to cultural studies, see Russell Berman, "Cultural Criticism and Cultural Studies," in R. B., *Cultural Studies of Modern Germany: History, Representation, and Nationhood* (Madison WI: U of Wisconsin P, 1993), 11-25.

14

Cross-Gendered Cross-Cultural Studies and the German Program

ALICE A. KUZNIAR
University of North Carolina, Chapel Hill

The premise underlying the argument presented here is that the German curriculum needs to wake up to the necessity of making what is taught and researched in our departments vital to the rest of the arts and humanities on campus, and not solely in the context of a connection to the German contingents in history and political science departments. That is to say, we need to contexualize our work in terms not of *German* Studies but *Cultural* Studies. Currently in our field a vast discourse pursues the issues of German nationalism and national identity, which—apart from obvious mammoth political developments in the Federal Republic—has conceivably arisen out of a need *in this country* to define German Studies. This discourse attempts to answer such questions as how and when a sense of German national identity was/is constituted, how it is upheld or modified in exile, how a national and cultural identity is premised on the exclusion of Others, whether Germany exists primarily as a cultural rather than political nation, or what the manifestations are of German colonialism. Despite the critical, deconstructive force behind these questions, I find it paradoxical that this very issue unwittingly reinforces our insular position in American academe by remaining German-focused. The fascination with nationality and nationalism is conceivably a factor of our teaching a national language and its customs (we don't teach Turkish) and our unease about potentially or unwittingly reinforcing an ideology of cultural distinctiveness and cohesiveness via this linguistic umbrella. Ironic, too, is the ability of this critical discourse on national identity to camouflage class and economic inequalities by attributing them to ethnic differences.

I am far from suggesting that courses on the problems of nationalism cannot be offered in terms that would attract other students from a Cultural Studies Program. But Cultural Studies is only in part involved with issues of the formation of cultural identity and imperialism; it also involves film and media studies, women's studies, gay and lesbian studies, for instance, and the intersections between them. In fact, where I want to end up in this paper is demonstrating how gay and lesbian studies can be instrumental in the project of denationalizing Germanistik. But what is my motivation behind advocating such a project? By aligning ourselves less with a "German-Studies" self-identity and more with a "Cultural Studies" networking, we can increase our visibility and prestige on campus as well as with university presses, hence before the wider academic community. This move is sorely needed not just to save our own jobs but, more importantly, to contribute to major debates in the arts and humanities. (I would even argue that hiring needs to be taken out of the hands of German departments for the purpose of furthering interdisciplinarity and the importance of cultural theory.) Although we have witnessed an exciting influx of various critical methodologies into our field (from anthropology, literary theory, feminist theory, philosophy, and so forth), we have not been active in feeding back into theoretical discourses at large. Moreover, with the demise of first DeMan and then deconstruction, we have lost any glamor and hence students that Hegel, Hölderlin, and Nietzsche once brought to our departments.

Part of our uncertainty about our role in the profession—to which the very existence of this conference attests—is that we sense how other fields view our work, and too often it is unjustly as a mere service department for foreign language acquisition. Yet perhaps we have ourselves to blame here, for by insisting on our students acquiring fluency we isolate and insulate our classes from other disciplines.

To be sure, by emphasizing the specificity and ultimate untranslatability of a foreign language, we teach respect for cultural differences. What, though, if we were to consider the practice in Asian Studies? Given the years needed to attain any degree of fluency in Chinese and Japanese, there is not the expectation that to take courses on Asian literature one needs to know the language. And, of course, it is Cultural Studies as a concept that has opened up this third literature and cinema for study at the American college. In other words, what I am suggesting by drawing on the Cultural Studies model is that we need to switch to teaching more courses that can offer texts in translation, despite the restriction the change will entail in the breadth of our syllabi. My experience has been that what I lose in terms of diversity or availability of German materials is more than made up by the other texts that can be introduced. For instance, in order both to attract students from other fields and to broaden the theoretical base of the German-department student I incorporate heavy doses of theory (and not just Frankfurt school, Luhmann, or Kittler). Such courses can then be cross-listed in other departments or described in a campus-wide Cultural Studies bulletin. My clientele for such courses has been on the average 50% German department students and 50% from elsewhere, including art history, communication studies, religious studies, and the various languages, including Classics. The influx of different students revitalizes the classes, and I feel that I am contributing more to a campus-wide intellectual endeavor.

Let me be more specific. A course on "psychoanalysis and literature" took several essays by Freud as a springboard for further readings from Derrida and Lacan to Kristeva, Irigaray, and Jessica Benjamin. A course on "Women in German Cinema" (taught at both the undergraduate and graduate level) simultaneously counted for the Women's studies major. It attracted a variety of students because it was the only course on campus dealing with women and film. To meet their needs, I had the students read several essays on feminist film theory. Unfortunately, my colleagues would not let this course be counted toward the German undergrad major because it was taught in English. This spring, I will offer a course on the Undead, from Romanticism (or Nekromantik, as I like to call it), Expressionist film, and Freud to contemporary vampire films. It is a class that deals with cult and occult literary and cinematic phenomenon. In the past, in a class that was made up exclusively from students outside German, I taught Wenders and Handke in the parameters of the postmodernist debate. We read such classic texts on postmodernism as Huyssen, Jameson, Baudrillard, and Habermas. Paradoxically, the nondepartmental students regarded Handke and Wenders as Americanized, whereas the German department students saw the two as marginal figures unworthy of study (we have a strongly survey-oriented curriculum). I therefore wonder to what extent we have indoctrinated our students to be blind to their own culture.

I am convinced that those of us in German have much to offer gay and lesbian studies too, but unfortunately this is an area whose territory is virtually unmapped. As I discovered in editing and researching *Outing Goethe and His Age*—to be published next year with Stanford University Press—any gay archeology can no longer afford to ignore the strong, unique German legacy that Winckelmann ushers in. His sensualized, homoerotic ideal of Classical beauty establishes a tradition momentarily inherited by Goethe and Hölderlin but in the long run repressed in the ascendency of a Kantian disinterested view of art. It resurfaces again, however, in the aesthetics of Wilde and Pater and more recently in Mapplethorpe's photography. Incidentally, the period we call the "Goethezeit" was termed by Goethe himself the "Century of Winckelmann" and by Kant the "Century of Frederick the Great"—a difference in terminology which attests to the lack of stigmatization attached to same-sex attraction during the 18th century. The important point is that appreciation of this difference needs to be taught in our classrooms, in part so that our current straight-jacketing notions of sexuality and gender—including our presumption about gay identity—can be called into question. Furthermore, a queerying of gender dichotomies promises to be indispensible for feminist scholarship, which—to its detriment—is caught up in male-female dualisms.

The importance of investigating a specifically German gay archeology doesn't stop with the Goethezeit, however. In her book *Tendencies*, Eve Segdwick observes how "Virtually all the competing, conflicting figures for understanding same-sex desire—archaic ones and modern ones, medicalized and politicizing, those emphasizing

pederastic relations, gender inversion, or 'homo-'homosexuality—
were coined and circulated in the first place in German, and through
German culture, medicine and politics" (66). The medical and legal
discourse on homosexuality she refers to was developed by German
sexologists in the last quarter of the 19th century. The term "homosexuality" was first coined in German in 1869 and wasn't imported
into the English language until the 1890s with a translation of Krafft-
Ebbing's *Psychopathia Sexualis*. The homosexual rights movement
was very strong in Germany in the early part of this century. Yet despite extensive historical studies on this period, there is a sad paucity
of works in German homosexual literary history (apart from Jim
Jones's work), an absence which is even more surprising given the
current popularity of queer theory.

Of course, German cinema is particularly queer. In 1919 a film
starring Conrad Veidt, Anita Berber, and Magnus Hirschfeld entitled
Anders als die Andern was made as a plea for tolerance for homosex-
uals. Lesbians even made it big time to the Weimar screen in *Die
Büchse der Pandora* and *Mädchen in Uniform*. Today the legacy of
Fassbinder continues in the work of Praunheim, Adlon, Treut, Ottinger, and numerous younger directors, such as Michael Stock, who
at the age of 25 directed an astonishing feature film, *Prinz in Hölle-
land*. Although queer German cinema has attracted some note by
scholars outside our immediate field, again next to nothing is being
done by German scholars. This problem is compounded in lesbian
studies. Apart from the work of Biddy Martin, lesbian issues are
hardly addressed, despite the strength and support of Women in German. I had a very difficult time finding even one contributor to the
Outing Goethe volume who would examine female passionate
friendships. Conceivably, the need to closet sexual orientation before
one's colleagues and students might be the reason behind this neglect, although it is ridiculous to think that one's scholarship in any
way betrays one's sexual practice.

I should like to come back to the issue of German nationality I
initially broached but do so via queer cinema. You might find the example I choose marginal or not generalizable enough, but Monika
Treut's work can be found at your local video store and thus is probably well enough known among video-literate young Americans

today—especially if they browse through the gay and lesbian section, which I bet they all do. Along with Rosa von Praunheim's *Überleben in New York*, Monika Treut's *Virgin Machine* and *My Father is Coming* stand in contrast to earlier German films such as Herzog's *Stroszek* or Wenders's *Alice in the Cities* and *The State of Things* that make the trip to the US appear like an exile. For Praunheim and Treut, the nationality of the female immigrant barely sets her apart in the multi-racial and multi-ethnic metropolis of New York. The crossing of cultural barriers then encodes a very natural crossing or obscuring of heterosexual gender boundaries. In fact, queer sexuality rather than nationality becomes the major (now positive) signifier of difference.

The story of *My Father is Coming* is this: Vicky, who waits tables and tries to land acting jobs, gets a visit from her rather overweight German father Hans. When he first arrives, he behaves like a stereotypical German tourist who comes to colonize and civilize America: he brings sausage in his suitcase and insists you can't find the likes of it in New York (of all places) and then asks if at least the water is potable. Yet the more obnoxiously he behaves as a foreigner, the more he is reminded by others of the Germans' Nazi past. Vicky, in the meantime, hits a streak of bad luck. While her father effortlessly lands a spot in a commercial, Vicky auditions in vain to get a part in Annie Sprinkle's new film *Pornutopia*, she then is torn in her amorous leanings: she finds herself attracted simultaneously to a handsome female-to-male transsexual and to her co-worker, a Puerto Rican woman named Lisa, who suffered abject poverty in childhood and now loves to eat. When her father discovers the two women in bed together, after Vicky has acted as if her gay roommate Ben were her husband, Hans disappears. After a kind of New Age sexual experience with Annie, the exposure to sex shops, and an encounter with a middle-aged guru who practices skin-piercing, Hans, espying Vicky in a bar, goes in to tell her he accepts her lifestyle. He toasts America and soon leaves for home sporting a baseball cap.

Jo, the transsexual, states that "people should have the choice to become who they are." One's past—whether it be one's nationality (Hans), class (Lisa), or even sex (Jo)—can be altered. Who a person is can never be taken for granted despite all appearances. In a scene in

Vicky's apartment, the camera pans across a poster of Marlene Dietrich in a man's suit: is this actress gay or straight, German or American? If sexuality isn't something given but something one becomes or acts out, then nationality too is a matter of performance. The opening sequence shows Vicky auditioning for a part as a German tourist in a Chinese restaurant and being coached to behave like a concentration *camp* commandant. The scene exposes American prejudices against Germans, yet it also suggests that national affiliation is a pose or put-on anyway. The film points out that in order to have your nationality recognized, you have to act it out. Thus Lisa, who speaks like a native New Yorker, says no one believes her when she says she is Puerto Rican. Hans's boorishness and heavy German accent make his adherence to his national identity look ridiculous. And in adopting American culture, Hans and Vicky make Americanisms—like the baseball cap—seem arbitrary. This is not to say that the film levels ethnic or cultural differences or is fundamentally indifferent to them, but that it plays up their queerness. This film portrays nationality, American as well as German, as a form of drag.

Significantly, neither Vicky nor Hans could pass as Americans, yet they can cross-over into the new culture. Rather than flawlessly imitating American speech, dress, or gestures, they retain the marks of cultural difference. Indeed, one could say that Treut has them adopting a nationality that is not their own in order to highlight and resignify these differences ironically.[1] The gap between performance and "original" clearly emphasizes that one is not what one performs, yet not in any negative sense. By the end of the film, Hans no longer takes for granted as natural and self-evident what we the viewers saw as arbitrary, namely his German prejudices against America. Instead, upon being exposed to the theatricality of porn and skin-piercing artists, Hans himself becomes accepting of and even playful with signifiers of identity. We the audience in turn become accepting of his overweight body and welcome, along with Annie Sprinkle, his ex-

---

[1] In her recent short *Taboo Parlor*, included in the omnibus film *Erotique* (1994), Treut continues this tradition of criss-crossing nationalities: her two lesbian characters speak English but live in Hamburg.

pressing sexual desire. In other words, the citationality of a national-istic mode of behavior that makes Hans look ridiculous does not have to be compulsory, as it is for him at the start of the film, but can be voluntary and playful.[2] Rejoicing at playing a part in a commerical and earning big bucks for it, Hans learns to cite and mime American custom with ease.[3] Nor is Hans's mimicry of American custom a question of assimilation, in other words, of his need to recognize himself in the signifiers of another culture and to remain in this country. That this does not occur is not a disappointment to him but rather a liberation from fixed identity categories, the source of judg-mental prejudice; hence he accepts his daughter's sexuality, which, significantly, is also not easily pigeonholed.

In her study in postmodern cross-culturalism Treut advocates a truly *queer nation*hood. Interestingly, many German films from Ul-rike Ottinger's *Madame X* and *Johanna d'Arc of Mongolia* to Mar-garethe von Trotta's *L'Africana*, Percy Adlon's *Salmonberries*, and Rosa von Praunheim's *Überleben in New York* show the lesbian liv-ing outside Germany. In the foreign land, one's search for identity leads neither back to one's cultural roots nor to adaptation and as-similation but to an allegiance to queerness, which is to say, to the productive dissonances in the cross-identifications that compose one's personality. The very word "queer" affirms both one's sexual and immigrant status as an outsider and marks them not as a stigma but as a performance and thus as a choice. Treut's immigrants do not so much discover a monolithic America and try to fit in to its social structure as they construct a community of another culture for them-selves. They (as well as we the viewer) see this country though their eyes. The paradigm for this queerying of national and cultural iden-tity is decidedly the receptivity Treut demonstrates to a range of sex-ual expression and experimentation.

---

[2] Here I am indebted to the distinctions Judith Butler draws in her discussion of gender performance in *Bodies that Matter: On the Discursive Limits of "Sex"* (New York: Routledge, 1993).

[3] Another example of compulsory citationality of ethnic affiliation that, however, is no less terrible for being performed occurs in the opening sequence when Vicky, in a casting tryout, is being coached to act the "typical" German, i.e., obnoxiously.

Treut's films thus can serve as a model for our situation as American "Germanisten" in their problematizing or queerying of German identity in a non-German context. Moreover, she encourages us and our American students to embrace new, foreign territories and bodies of knowledge. It goes without saying that I believe it is these lesbian, cross-cultural, subtitled films that we should be teaching. Let's embrace an Act-Up Now Agenda for the 21st Century!

15

"Everyman His Own Cultural Historian": German Studies and the Limits of Competence

FRANK TROMMLER
University of Pennsylvania

This is a short comment on the place and substance of German Studies in relationship to the traditional offerings of German departments. A conference on the present state of our profession in the United States might allow a somewhat critical reexamination of the much heralded German Studies. As generally agreed, German Studies have enriched the program of numerous departments in the past fifteen years, attracted a new group of students, and generated a momentum for younger faculty to engage in cultural and interdisciplinary studies. My comments will address this new engagement of younger faculty in cultural—i.e. not just linguistic and literary—studies. My remarks will focus on 1) the competence for these studies and 2) the place of German Studies within the traditional structures of German as part of the American academy.

I

"Everyman His Own Cultural Historian" is a take-off on the famous presidential address which the eminent American historian Carl Becker delivered to the American Historical Association in 1931. The speech was entitled, "Everyman His Own Historian," typically reflecting the male orientation that until recently was the rule

in history as well as in other academic disciplines. Despite this gen-
der-centrism, the title of the speech has been quoted ever since as it
provides a neat expression of a democratizing tendency in a discipline that was known for its rigid professionalism. Whoever is familiar with history as a discipline knows that much of this
professionalism had come from Germany where the standards of
Leopold Ranke and Theodor Mommsen, the insistence on working
from documents, archives, and sources, had reigned supreme.

Carl Becker was a very knowledgeable, sometimes friendly,
sometimes unfriendly critic of Germany and this particular trait of
its historians. In his speech he made the historical inquiry compatible with the thinking of a broader public, even extracted part of his
definition from the everyday use of history by Mr. Everyman. Based
on the belief that a fact is not something objective and material in
the outer world, but only something the mind is convinced is true,
Becker asserted that Mr. Everyman, in his sense of history, was not
far from the professional for whom, however, it was much more difficult to arrive at this historical relativism. The reconstruction of the
historical dimension—today we would say: the contextualization of
documents—Becker maintained, is a popular practice. By taking the
liberty to extend his famous line to "Everyman His Own Cultural
Historian," I hope to connect his democratizing thinking with the
current trend toward cultural studies.

Everyone his or her own cultural historian: considering the enormous expansion of cultural history and cultural studies in recent
years, one cannot but sense a liberating spirit in this motto, liberating as it helps to open up historical perspectives beyond the strict
canon of literary criticism. I am committed to this approach as part
of our teaching and research agenda. It has helped me find conceptu-
alizations of literary texts that allowed new readings of these texts
and provided new sparks both in classroom understanding and published scholarship.

Carl Becker articulated an entertaining plea for democratizing
historiography. However, he did not go as far as letting Mr. Everyman
decide the nature and goal of the historian's work. In this and other
equally entertaining essays, Becker insists on clear professional standards, even when he labels the historian a "keeper of myths" and as-

serts: "Our proper function is not to repeat the past but to make use of it, to correct and rationalize for common use Mr. Everyman's mythological adaptation of what actually happened."[1] Becker clearly insists on the differences between professional academic work and Mr. Everyman's mythologizing of interesting experiences. He distinguishes rigorously between a historical fact and the event which it symbolized. While he is surprisingly close to current assertions of historical relativity, he is not relativizing the quality standards of original research which should accompany the teaching of students in the classroom. This should give us pause when we immerse ourselves in new methodological ventures, be it the turn to social history, the turn to feminism, the linguistic turn, the turn to comparative literature, the turn to multiculturalism, all of which have revitalized the study of German language, culture, and literature.

This revitalization developed as a struggle against the perception of German departments as ancillary fixtures in the academy. The fight has led to a feeling of empowerment over the mere fulfillment of teaching quotas. It has raised both the intellectual level and the emotional commitment in a discipline that dwells on the fringes of the humanities in America. It has often been said that a small discipline is much more open to interdisciplinary ventures than large disciplines. No wonder, at the margins other territories are more visible, though not necessarily easier to grasp. The discussion on interdisciplinarity has helped shape institutional practices of German Studies, for instance in the German Studies Association.

In contrast, Martin Mueller remarked that the interdisciplinary ventures in the much larger English departments tended to be an intradepartmental affair:

The English department is frequently the largest department in a university. In a sizable university, members of English departments have a hard time engaging in sustained interaction with

[1] Carl Becker, *Everyman His Own Historian: Essays on History and Politics* (Chicago, 1966), 253.

members of other departments: they are kept busy by professional obligations within their departments. In such a situation there is a very strong tendency for interdisciplinary work to reconstitute itself as a departmental subdiscipline. The not entirely happy result is intradepartmental interdisciplinary work.[2]

This assessment, articulated in the late 1980s, has become even more important in the mid-1990s when English departments threaten to swallow up the discussion on multiculturalism without much interchange with foreign language departments that actually present the study of other cultures.

These developments need to be closely observed. There are good arguments to be made about the provincialism of much of the debate about multiculturalism as it tends to express the intracultural problems of English departments. After these departments had thrown out the study of American culture in the heyday of New Criticism, they had a hard time reintegrating contextual reading, methodological diversity, cultural studies. Since the late 1980s the wheel of confronting the 'other' world is being reinvented—often at the expense of the foreign language departments. To these departments, especially the German departments, the invention of New Historicism looked like an example of this reinvention. Given the history-laden nature of their material, they felt less need than new historicists to rescue "their own discipline from the aridity of a strict formalism—of both the New Critical and the poststructuralist stripes—by a reopening of contextual inquiry."[3] The expansion of German Studies since the 1970s was itself a reflection of the growing interest in contextualizing the study of German language and literature.

And yet, Muller's general critique of the common interdisciplinary practice as an intradisciplinary practice can also be applied outside of English departments. His characterization of the process is telling:

[2] Martin Mueller, "Yellow Stripes and Dead Amarillos," *Profession 89* (1989): 26.
[3] John H. Zammito, "Are We Being Theoretical Yet? The New Historicism, the New Philosophy of History, and 'Practicing Historians,'" *Journal of Modern History* 65 (1993): 786.

Scholars get interested in a field outside [...] and read in it, perhaps even read widely in it. They get colleagues to become interested in the field. They start an MLA session, and they begin to publish articles, typically in literary journals that are for the most part refereed by literary scholars. The work may be good or bad, but it rarely results from intense interaction with practitioners of the other discipline, and it is typically not refereed or reviewed by those practitioners.[4]

Take, for instance, the urge of many Germanists to write about the social and political effects of German unification, effects for which they do not find enough documentation in literary works. Or take the interest in the social history of modern Germany as an analogous enterprise to writing German literary history. Or the interest in historiography itself as an endeavor that has become the subject of debates about rhetorical and literary emplotment strategies. Examples for transgressing the boundaries of literary criticism abound. German Studies would not have expanded without this impetus. However, does enthusiasm make up for lack of competence? Does the reading of the U.S. edition of *Die Zeit* qualify as the basis for a scholarly article on the changes in intellectual life after the fall of the Wall?

Having promoted interdisciplinary German Studies myself, I am aware of the vulnerability of the concept as an agenda for scholarly work. Yet, I maintain that this vulnerability cannot be diminished by a comprehensive theory of German Studies. Only a superior practice can do it. In other words, the concept will continue to attract all kinds of accusations, often from within the German departments; the only way to counteract them is with quality. Scholarly quality is conditioned by an intact peer-review process, by the accountability of the disciplinary transgressions, and by effective models both at conference sessions and in publications. Conceptualized as a *Haltung*, an attitude that can be learned,[5] interdisciplinarity helps to redefine the

---

[4] Mueller, "Yellow Stripes," 27.

[5] Frank Trommler, "The Future of German Studies or How to Define Interdisciplinarity in the 1990s," *German Studies Review* 15 (1992): 201-17.

discipline, something that Lynn Hunt, one of the leading scholars of cultural studies, considers an important stimulus for the history profession.[6]

Quality in scholarship, an admittedly difficult concept, is closely related to the admittedly difficult concept of truth-finding. This concerns literary texts as well as cultural contexts. Once more a thought by Carl Becker: he took repeated pleasure in pointing out that so many scholars have been satisfied too soon. If it is so, it might be that satisfaction is not the most relevant consideration to associate with truth-finding. Indeed, we are often dissatisfied with our work on texts. However, that should not make our scholarship solely dependent on the satisfaction that the brush with other academic fields provides. The consequences are too dangerous: if cultural studies are lacking in scholarly quality, they will disappear fast. If they are there only to fulfill the requirements of personal or group satisfaction, they will make the concept 'cultural studies' useless as a viable guide for students of German. Cultural interests can be satisfied elsewhere by way of immersing oneself in today's TV learning channels, computer information packages, and general journalism.

Enough said. I plead for the use of cultural studies in the field of German, yet in a balance with the existing scholarly, institutional, and budgetary setup that has proven to be maintained as part of the American university and college agenda.

II

At a conference that was organized to rethink and clarify the investment of Americans in the study of German, it seems appropriate to turn the attention also to the traditions within which this endowment has been treated. We cannot separate our work in German from the intellectual developments in American higher education and the political constellations on both sides of the Atlantic. One point seems particularly important for a realistic assessment: the intellec-

---

[6] Lynn Hunt, "The Virtues of Disciplinarity," *Eighteenth-Century Studies* 28 (1994):1-7.

tual and cultural development of the United States in the major part of the twentieth century has been dominated by the desire to build a strong and identifiable, yet open American culture which can compete with European cultures and even exert leadership in the world. It has been an immensely broad and dynamic endeavor which has drawn extensively on English sources and personnel, wrenching leadership in the arts away from France, and in positioning America as the victorious heir to Weimar culture, German modernism, and European scientific achievements.

Germany played a role in this endeavor. Of course, in two wars it was the enemy, a factor in shaping this cultural consolidation. But it also remained the country that had provided important models for the American concept of higher education and the use of culture as a unifying symbol of identity since the nineteenth century. We cannot overlook these traditions that have given our discipline as well as the German section in the history departments a small yet secure place in higher education. This is not rhetoric. It was, of course, only partially *Germanistik* in the German configuration of the discipline. When Johns Hopkins, the University of Pennsylvania, Yale, and Cornell bestowed Ph.D.s in German after the 1870s, our early colleagues saw the mission of the departments, which had grown out of the language institutes and old philologies, as establishing beachheads for the impressive accomplishments of German literature and culture in the centers of American learning. The mission was not only to encourage the study of classical German texts by such writers as Goethe and Schiller, but also to contribute to the concept of a comprehensive education (*Bildung*), and to nurture the emergence of a genuinely national culture as an engrossing and unifying factor in the building of a modern America.

The other impulse derived from German ideas on how to unify a nation took hold in the discipline of History. In the second half of the nineteenth century, historians who had learned their craft in German universities (mainly Berlin and Heidelberg) such as George Bancroft developed a historiography of the United States exemplifying its unified state. So strong was the unifying tendency that the advocates of a more diversified view, ironically including many German-Americans, never quite succeeded in finding a national audience for their ethno-oriented historiography.

Looking at the conditions under which the field was taught and financed even during the World Wars, we should be aware that the main contribution from Germany has always been both as unifying *and* diversifying factor in establishing American identity, with the proviso that learning about the German experience also meant learning about ourselves. Even if at this moment the arguments for a harmonizing and unifying view of American society and culture are being labeled conservative, we cannot all of a sudden deny this side of our heritage in the academy. This heritage provides a long-term rationale for the funding of German even if we develop a new focus on German Studies as the investigation of the other and use it to teach European cultures as models of otherness. German studies can flourish as an integral part of and even beyond the traditional setup, as an indispensable enhancement of the department's contribution to the home institution. However, it can do so only if the department retains an emphasis on the competent teaching of language, on transmitting cultural literacy, and—as the ultimate professional goal—communicating linguistic and cultural fluency. The reason for this restriction seems to me to be closely tied to the established lines of budgetary authorization.

The young Ph.D. who leaves her alma mater, having successfully landed a teaching position at another institution (most likely at a smaller college) will draw much of her or his everyday identity on teaching the language and teaching it well. However, beyond absolving his or her apprenticeship successfully, the agenda is theoretically wide open. As the discussion concerning the pragmatics of German Studies at the recent conference of the German Studies Association has shown, he or she might face classes where students are intent on reading literature rather than political or historical documents in German. He or she might also face the situation whereby students of German develop a greater interest in the plight of East Germans subjected to Western consumerism and Western arrogance, foregoing the ambition of reading Rilke's poems in the original. In both cases, the assistant professor should have been provided with the expertise not only to respond to these desires, but also to respond to them well. This means being able to teach the students to open up to aspects of the other, be it reading poems by Rilke and Hofmannsthal or discussing gender and race issues in the German context. To achieve this goal and ensure this balance is, I think, the best investment in the future as we approach the twenty-first century.

16

DAAD Symposium
A Protocol

TODD C. HANLIN
University of Arkansas

Defining the Problem

Co-hosts John A. McCarthy and Richard A. Zipser welcomed the participants and introduced the theme "prospects for change—changing our prospects." At a time of increasing foreign-language enrollments nationally, German is experiencing an apparent decline in the number of its students. To what could this decline be attributed? And what, if anything, can Germanists do to stem the loss of future students?

As a point of departure, A. Leslie Wilson and John Van Cleve summarized their recent book *Remarks on the Needed Reform of German Studies in the USA* and enumerated several "problems": a lack of definition and consistency between various programs of German; the disparity of native-born and—educated Germans within a uniquely American educational system; the isolation of language teachers from those who "profess" literature or culture; American Germanists whose focus and attention is set on Europe, not on America; a professional language of communication (German) which isolates us from English-speaking colleagues in different disciplines with whom we share common intellectual interests.

Professional Profile

Based on the 1992 AATG membership survey, a statistical overview of the profession is now possible; the available data prompt the following suggestions for improving or strengthening enrollments, given recent trends:

1)Emphasize German study in the primary and secondary schools, and foster collaboration with post-secondary institutions;

2) Increase study abroad for both students and teachers;

3) Introduce "German across the curriculum" wherever possible;

4) Encourage the cooperation with and the continued development of more and different disciplines;

5) Introduce different "tracks" for language students of varied abilities and interests;

6) Increase links with colleagues in primary and secondary schools to learn how to improve teacher recruitment and training; to support outreach programs for schools.

The question of what standards and levels of proficiency are appropriate for German students nationwide remains unanswered. Perceived weaknesses in recent PhD recipients lead to the conclusion that they are well educated as Germanists, but not well trained as professionals. The question arose whether there aren't too many PhD programs nationally, unethically over-producing graduates, who have no realistic chance for university employment. Perhaps the establishment of a "National Council of Graduate Programs in German" could informally solve this dilemma, coordinating PhD production to meet perceived need, and also deciding what our graduates should learn or know. Further suggestions for alleviating this problem were: to oppose hiring foreign-trained scholars until the job shortage is relieved, and to oppose graduate programs that are populated primarily with students imported from European universities. However, there was equally strong sentiment that we should avoid quotas on the production of new PhDs and allow the market and/or the students themselves to decide the issue.

Visibility in the Academy

Reflecting the diversity in higher education nationwide, each of our individual programs defies standardized definitions or norms. Therefore we each must "make" our own visibility vis-a-vis our respective student bodies, our colleagues in other departments, the administration, indeed the institution as a whole. Significantly, we must educate both colleagues and administrators to appreciate our contributions to the institution if we wish to enjoy their appreciation and support in the future. Since quality teaching attracts students, we should also constantly strive to improve our instructional skills. In addition, we should teach introductory and interdisciplinary courses to expose undergraduates to our field; to this end, we should form alliances with colleagues in related disciplines to offer team-taught courses.

Americanization of the Undergraduate Curriculum

With the realization that Germanics may be expendable at many institutions during budget crises, we must solidify our enrollments. To this end, we must know our students and understand their perception(s) of German; many feel that German is not "sexy," is difficult to learn, and may be of little practical value in the future. We must understand these stereotypes if we hope to combat them; we must "fine-tune" our message and "market" our discipline in a more attractive way.

In other academic settings, "high culture" may have to defer to a goals-based curriculum—simply attracting new students may be the greatest challenge. We must be flexible and resourceful in our approach—we may have to "grow our own" students. Some suggestions included advertising double-majors for students in foreign languages, arranging student travel opportunities and lecture programs (with simultaneous translations and a free lunch for all students attending!), satellite broadcasts of German programming available in public areas on campus (as required viewing and as assigned homework). Those who have chosen German as a major may be encouraged to do business or technical translations under faculty supervision for practice and to enhance their CVs. Internships with local German businesses, teaching-enhancement workshops, and an "open-house" policy for visiting high school groups can also expand outreach and thus enrollments. Still other universities have developed unique or specialized programs to meet perceived student needs or demands, such as the international engineering program at Rhode Island, international business at South Carolina, etc.

In summary, the participants perceived no apparent commonality among our various curricula—and also apparently desired none.

Americanization of the Graduate Curriculum

Our graduate programs have become alienated from the undergraduate curricula, resulting in a chaotic variety of course offerings. We must ultimately persuade our institutions of the necessity of including Germanics in the graduate curriculum, based on our contribution to cultural knowledge. In curricular matters, we must emphasize Germany within a European context, and in future staffing we should take care to hire faculty with interdisciplinary interests, thereby enhancing our visibility and flexibility toward other disciplines. To this end, we should change the undergraduate curriculum from communication skills to pre-lit, and develop our course offerings for non-majors.

Here one participant felt that the proliferation of multi-disciplinary courses certainly makes prospective graduate students "more interesting," but that there is no substitute for a standardized canon and a traditional background in literature and civilization. To improve our graduate programs, we must emphasize historical knowledge (i.e., literary periodization) as the basis for our curricula, complemented by disciplinary breadth. We should strive for coherence in "interpretation" and critical thought, and should foster writing as a critical skill, required for all seminars.

Another participant felt that the purpose of graduate study in Germanics should be to mediate German culture for an American audience, to "popularize" in the best sense of the word. We may need to differentiate our graduate programs, specializing in distinct areas or general periods (such as "1750 to the Present," with the attendant exclusion of depth in earlier languages and periods). Too, the old canon may need up-dating to reflect our contemporary activities as "Modern German Studies."

Multiperspectivism

One participant saw overemphasis on national literatures as the result of an over-focus on nationalism, thus the reduced interest in German literature, relatively speaking. The current preference for foreign-language fluency precludes an interconnectedness with external disciplines. Expanded multi-perspectivistic courses and cultural studies offer renewed hope for attracting students.

Another participant agreed, however, that cultural relativity should not replace research relativity or creativity. Regardless of the approach, quality in scholarship is of primary importance; indeed, the "core," the traditional and historical mission of U.S. colleges should be maintained.

One response posited our common mission as developing an American audience for German Studies, much as British Germanists did during the 1950s and 1960s. Rather than communicating only with each other (often in incomprehensible jargon) at conferences and in our German-language journals, focusing our dialogue on European colleagues and publications, we should attempt to reach out in English, to colleagues in other disciplines, to literate citizens and students who would appreciate and benefit from our knowledge.

Publishing

The editors of various professional journals shared their related concerns, such as the dilemma of publishing articles either exclusively in English or in both English and German to facilitate communication with interested readers in other academic disciplines, and the as-yet unforeseeable impact of electronic publishing on the future of all journals.

Action Agenda for the 21st Century

The most refreshing session of the entire symposium was provided by three graduate students from Vanderbilt University. They shared with their elders their unique experiences and observations, their hopes and fears for the future of Germanics. Some suggestions included: a merit system to reward excellent teaching; practical experience in teaching literature to complement their apprenticeship in the language classroom; the funding of fewer students over a longer period of time during their graduate careers; statements from graduate programs declaring the placement results of recent graduates; the pursuit of other employment options for graduates beyond academe; the appointment of a graduate representative to the departmental curriculum committee. Moreover, all concluded that discussions such as those evident at this symposium should be continued on a regular basis.

In an attempt to establish a agenda for the professions, numerous individual responses were noted; it was felt that we, as a profession, must:

• Examine and strengthen the place of German in our public school systems, beginning with the earliest grades; lobby on their behalf to ensure government funding for these programs. We must support public schools to ensure our own future.

• Make a conscious effort to share our own university resources (films, realia, etc.) with our colleagues in the local public schools.

• Support ACTFL/AATG in their national lobbying efforts, while cooperating on the local level to effect reforms or improvements.

• Remember our professional ethos—that our primary obligation is to teach our students. We must overcome the dichotomy between teachers and researchers, and foster a loyalty to the profession as a whole, while resisting parochial instincts of self-survival.

• Accept the fact that diversification will continue; nevertheless we must also retain a "center," a "core discipline" with which we can identify, around which we can rally.

• Expand the profession through translation of business and legal documents, as well as of literary texts.

• Foster a cosmopolitan discourse, rather than limit it to an American perspective alone; also promote "interesting" aspects of German studies with enthusiasm, to reach untapped studet audience.

• Identify our "service region" to identify our prospective student populations in recruitment efforts.

• Identify and explore other career options for PhDs in German.

• Use interdisciplinary cultural studies courses as an introduction to our discipline, as well as the present path through language study.

• Improve our academic visibility and exposure on our own campuses; educate administrative officers, accept administrative duties to influence/effect our position; *we* should initiate new ideas for reform.

• Examine the number and quality of PhD programs, pool our resources, and reduce the total number of new PhDs to relieve the job market crunch.

• Attract and retain the new breed of "minority" students (Asian-Americans, African-Americans, etc.) who have traditionally not chosen to study German.

• Investigate "German-American" studies as a new avenue for expansion in German, likewise Gender Studies, Lesbian Studies, cultural studies in general.

• Encourage "unpleasant ideas." Moreover, we have no right to complain about the direction of the profession, if we are not willing to work for change ourselves.

• Realize that the German language is our common identity, while also recognizing that no single approach or focus will work for all institutions. We must also celebrate our differences and the variety of strengths we bring to the profession, despite our national, gender, or generational differences.

In conclusion, we must continue to discuss these issues, while publicizing the positive aspects of Germanics as well.

17

An Outsider's View:
Concluding Remarks on the Occasion of the
DAAD Symposium: "Germanistik in the USA"

WILFRIED KRUG
German Embassy

While I have the floor, here is my contribution to the "Action Agenda" (it's up to you to judge whether this is a "cannonball" or more like a stray bullet): being an economist, it is my impression that we are somewhat underrepresented among germanists, historians, political scientists and others who are already very active in German Studies. Thus, I would like to suggest to try to achieve increased involvement of economists in German Studies endeavors. I think that more contributions by economists could be potentially valuable additions to analysis and teaching of quite a number of Germany-related issues, e.g. German unification and European integration.

I would like to thank John McCarthy and Richard Zipser for inviting me to this conference, and for entrusting me with the challenging task of delivering concluding remarks.

I would also like to thank everyone present, and indeed all members of the American Germanistik/Germanics/German Studies profession for the heartfelt welcome that you have consistently offered me ever since I walked into the first AATG meeting that I attended, in 1991. Although I'm not in your profession, and I cannot claim intellectual contributions to your work, I have always felt that you have included me in your discourse openly, and in a spirit of mutual trust.

You will not be surprised by the disclaimer that the views that I'm expressing or have expressed are entirely my own, and do not represent views of the German Embassy or of anyone else; therefore, if you feel I've made errors or misjudgments, these are also entirely my own, and I would of course appreciate any commments from your side.

It is impossible to sum up the conference in five minutes—I'll leave that to John and Richard—but I would like to share briefly with you some impressions and what I feel I have learned these past few days.

1. I am very impressed with your outstanding dedication, which I have witnessed here, to the profession (you can see that I am deliberately avoiding the issue of whether the profession should be called Germanics, Germanistics, Germanistik, German Studies or anything else), in spite of many problems, obstacles and probably also frustration that have to be overcome every day.

2. In what was said at this conference, I have consistently felt expressed your deep conviction that for American students, it is a worthwhile and gratifying endeavor to study and to be exposed to the German language, and to German and European things in general. According to what I've understood here, you feel that this is worthwhile not primarily because of abstract ideals of international understanding, but because it concretely enriches the student's lives and helps them to grow, to learn more about themselves, their country, their history, and many other important things. Differently from what the "Frankfurter Allgemeine Zeitung" reported about the recent Germanistentag in Aachen/Germany in September, 1994, I have detected at the present conference a strong sense as to what the goal of the profession in educating students should be.

3. I have felt expressed here a strong awareness that, in this endeavor of educating students, teaching about Germany means teaching about a fascinating (even the word "sexy" was used here), but also very complex culture (not to mention our language which often also is regarded as very complex). I realize that this endeavor calls for special efforts at a time when, on both sides of the Atlantic, young

people increasingly seem to expect instant gratification, thirty-second soundbites, and easy solutions for everything within no more than the duration of a sitcom episode. I am confident that it will be possible for you to continue to master the delicate balance between amounts of "Angst" and of "Fahrvergnügen" in the context of teaching about Germany, in view of different, sometimes maybe even conflicting goals, such as for example, "truth finding," searching for the scientifically best approaches to the analysis of phenomena, and attracting and motivating students.

4. I have gained very valuable hands-on insight into what the diversity of American postsecondary institutions means in practice for your profession (I like the phrase I picked up here: "There is no U.S. higher education system, but it works"). This diversity is of course quite different from the less varied German system within which "Germanisten" in Germany operate. Seen in reference to this background, I have realized that no matter what kind of institution a professor teaches at, there is a very substantial impact that he or she can make, at his or her institution, with teaching German and teaching about Germany and Europe, as has been shown during this conference.

5. I am leaving this conference with increased awareness of a number of sensitive dichotomies that seem to exist within the profession:

- American-born versus native speakers,
- research universities versus land-grant colleges,
- postsecondary versus pre-collegiate education,
- Germanistik versus Germani(sti)cs versus culture studies versus language studies,
- graduate versus undergraduate
- content versus language
- teaching versus research,

and maybe others that I forget to mention. I cannot offer solutions—it would probably constitute hermeneutical hubris to try to do so. But I would like to express the hope that these dichotomies—sometimes, if not "walls in the head," maybe "fences in the head," to use a "topos" familiar in analyses about Germany—can be dealt with in the spirit of a fruitful dialectic process, in the interest of the students and of the profession. (I have noted here with interest that some U.S. institutions have found their own, imaginative and forward-looking solution to the "American-born vs. native speaker" dichotomy by hiring British-or Turkish-born Germanists who of course are neither in the American-born nor in the native-speaker category).

Being the last of the invited participants to have the floor, I do feel that I can speak for everyone present in one respect:

- I would like to thank John McCarthy and Richard Zipser for the initiative for this conference, dedicated to enhancing the future of the profession, and for organizing and implementing it. Also, my special thanks to the graduate students for all the hands-on work that they did.
- I would like to thank Vanderbilt University, the University of Delaware, and the other contributors for their very gracious hospitality. I think that you have set precedents for future conferences in the profession, especially with the dinners and the sumptuous coffee breaks.

Preparing future generations for tomorrow's "global village" cannot be done by politicians just by giving speeches. It cannot be done by bureaucrats (like me) just by sometimes writing such speeches. It can only be achieved by educators—that's you.

Thank you, and the best wishes to all of you!

18

A Student's View

KATRIN SCHNEIDER
Vanderbilt University

I will present here two graduate-student perspectives; I speak both as a graduate student and as a student from Germany studying in the US. To make my position clearer, I would like to compare my current situation to the one I came from.

I started my studies at the Ludwig-Maximilians-Universität in Munich. Three years ago when I left for the States 7,500 students were enrolled in the German Department. One of the main reasons for that is that German students do not have to pay tuition. Thus a lot of people who do not know what to do, think: "Well, I know German anyway, I do not really have to study that." And they enroll in German. Although there is a decent number of professors, assistants and so on, the courses are over-crowded. More than 100 applicants must take a test to demonstrate knowledge of a text before being accepted into a class of forty. And that is a 'Hauptseminar,' a graduate student course. I admit that the situation is not like that in all courses but definitely in popular fields like the literature of the 20th century. A major difference in the German system lies in the disconnectedness of the professor's status at a school from his/her student's evaluations, simply because such evaluations do not exist. So, there is no control mechanism; that allows professors to stay at a god-like distance from their students, it means that students are entirely dependent on their professors' good-will.

That has an effect on the student's career as well. You have to stand out among literally thousands to be noticed by a professor. You should know from the first semester with whom you want to work. That affects an important aspect of the student's attitudes in class: you do not attend to learn something you did not know before, but to show off your knowledge. Because of that you do not admit even to other students your unsatisfactory knowledge in some things and you never ask for help as you do not want to embarrass yourself. One can imagine the effect on competition and motivation.

Now let me contrast that to our situation here. The points I make shall not only illustrate the specific attraction an American institution has for students from Germany but the positive aspects of the work atmosphere as a graduate student in general.

- The first but not the main issue is funding, which is basically non-existent in Germany. Most of us in our department at Vanderbilt have scholarships, that allow us to fully concentrate on our studies and participate in other related events and committees on campus. We can spend more time with each other and develop a sense of student community (that might sometime in the future be a community of professors).
- We are 17 graduate students with 6 professors at Vanderbilt. We know one another and in turn are known by others. That allows us not only to develop gradually in consultation with professors an interest in a topic or field but it reduces as well the level of nervousness before exams, because a complete stranger is not posing the questions.
- A large class consists of 12 students. Anything one has to say matters. And we all get the opportunity to articulate our ideas.
- The school provides us with high-tech facilities: computers, the internet, and a good library system (though not to be compared with the famous Staatsbibliothek in Munich, where the existence of books remains a mystery most of the time for "students only"). That keeps us up-to-date with what is going on in other institutions. At an early stage of our careers we are able to gain insight into the relationships among schools that

becomes essential when we enter the job-market.

- We have the opportunity of teaching which plays a major role in decisions for our professional futures. At this point I want to add—and this is just my own personal opinion—that I think first-year graduate students should have the possibility to teach. We here at Vanderbilt take not only a teaching methods course in our first semester but also enjoy the special support and guidance of our language supervisor. Maybe one could find a way of testing the personal abilities and aptitudes of a graduate student for teaching and make the methods course optional. But if one is eager and enthusiastic about teaching, why inhibit this source of energy which certainly would be appreciated by the undergraduate students? A funded semester without teaching might be more helpful for us later in the program, before our preliminary exams.
- The value of giving a paper at a conference or a symposium cannot be overestimated. We get the practical experience of talking to a professional audience, we are taken seriously, get involved in discussions with specialists from all over the country, and thereby begin to create our necessary job-search network.
- Last, but definitely not least, studying German literature in the US in a German/American-mixed classroom provides us all with two important perspectives: a critical distance to the country and literature that we study and the native-German insight. We all gain a new angle from a different educational system and cultural context; this makes German Studies bicultural studies.

After all that has been said about the role of German students in the States I feel I have to underscore the benefits we bring to this country. To put it succinctly: we make a distant country more concrete by being here. More specifically:

- Undergraduates and their paying parents appreciate having at some point in their education a native German teacher.
- Some of the American graduate students did not have the possi-

bility before to meet their peers from Germany.

- We attend regularly the activities of our foreign-language dormitory such as dinners with German conversation, sports-events and so on to share informally the German language and culture with undergraduate students outside the classroom. In our capacities as both teachers and students, we can provide undergraduate students with valuable insights into graduate student life (where they might be in the not too distant future) and we can give them the experience of a close-knit German department student body comprised of both undergraduates and graduates.
- We offer as well our services to the community by visiting high-school or elementary-school classrooms as native sources of information or simply by presenting a German table at an international fair. I think it is especially important for young students there (maybe future prospects for some German department?) to experience the teamwork of US and German students of German.

This brings me to my final point: How do I picture our future that has been so pessimistically painted at this symposium? I certainly think we have to work all together to increase undergraduate enrollment. I mentioned above some activities that graduate students can especially fulfill in their position as being just a little older than their undergraduate students.

There is, however, yet another topic that is essential to the future of the graduate students and, if worked out well, might at the same time attract undergraduates to major in German and maybe even continue later as graduate students themselves: we need opportunities to increase our market-value.

1. We should be allowed to teach literature as well as language courses to broaden our experiences.

2. Sometimes the courses offered for graduate students do not optimally prepare us with both broad and in-depth knowledge in our field, like period courses and historical overviews versus special topic and author courses. To prevent a deficiency in either of them I rec-

ommend a lecture series that would run and rerun every four years to provide the overview. I also urge the participation of a graduate student on the curricular committee of the department to be able to voice the research interests of the graduate students.

3. An essential tool would be work-shops to help train students to find a job. They should explain how to create a good personalized curriculum vitae, write cover letters, determine what writing-samples to include, reveal the main sources of job information, and offer mock-interviews.

4. In Germany we had to change our attitude towards job expectations long ago. Maybe Germans are in general more pessimistic than Americans. We cannot focus on one dream job, we have to be flexible and take into consideration that we may have to work somewhere else than at a university, such as in publishing, advertising or in totally different areas. So it is important to get as many feet in as many doors as we can—even while we are still students. I am thinking here of internships, summer jobs, and so on. The university could help establish closer ties to major companies in the immediate area and beyond to allow undergraduates and graduates the opportunity for "outside" work experiences. That would contribute to both the practical work experience of German majors and make them more visible to companies while combatting the image of Germans as being cerebral head-people. This might be a long shot, but a changed image might, in fact, attract more undergraduates to enroll in German when they recognize the value of their studies.

A lot has been said about graduate students from Germany invading the States as students and then as professors. My final point is to argue that a German graduate student in the US has basically three major ways to go after graduating, which should make clear that studying in the US does not include an easy ticket to paradise. If we go back to Germany it will be difficult to get full credit for our degrees unless we are supported by an international scholarship such as DAAD or Fulbright. If we return to the German free economy—our American degrees will sometimes be cherished—though not likely for studying literature. A major publishing company in München told me only this past summer that being almost bilingual would be very welcome since license-trading back and forth between German- and English-speaking countries is a growing part of the market. We, of course, could stay in the United States to teach. In my opinion a healthy mixture of Germans and Americans is as important for students as for professors. A lot has been said here about the (miserable) job prospects for graduate students. Let me throw the problem back to you: what else would you recommend for us to study or do? Today it is difficult to find a job anywhere. You have to be good, enthusiastic, with ideas and interests that show your future promise, and you have to be able to sell yourself. In that sense a university interview is not that different from a business one. The only bigger problem Germans face here, one that has been mentioned before and which our American counterparts face when they seek work in Germany (a possibility not discussed at all at this symposium) is how to get the visa to be allowed to stay!

19

An Organizer's View

RICHARD A. ZIPSER
University of Delaware

A few months before the Vanderbilt symposium on "Germanistik in the USA: Prospects for Change—Changing our Prospects," John McCarthy asked two other participants and me to prepare position papers on its significance. His plan was to use our statements to stimulate discussion at the conference as well as for publicity purposes, so that the academic community at Vanderbilt would know why we were gathering and what some of us were hoping to achieve. My contribution, written in September, 1995, follows under the title "Forethoughts."

This September, almost a full year after the symposium, John asked me to compose a retrospective on the Vanderbilt conference, indicating the extent to which it met my expectations, where it fell short, and what impact it has had to date on Germanistik in the USA. This second contribution is entitled "Afterthoughts."

Forethoughts

For me, the key to the future success of Germanistik in the USA lies in the word "change." I am convinced that major changes are necessary in the way German is taught and what students of German are taught, especially at the college and university level, if Germanistik (or German Studies) is to thrive as a discipline in the 21st century. I am therefore hopeful that the following three things will occur at the symposium: first that everyone attending will agree at the outset that Germanistik in this country is in desperate need of reform; second, that we will be able to reach agreement during the course of the symposium on the areas most in need of change and also try to formulate some realistic reform measures; and third, that everyone attending will return to his or her home institution and state with a new sense of professional purpose and missionary zeal.

Well, what needs to be changed? To begin with, I think that Germanists teaching at the college and university level have to establish much closer ties—formally and informally—with those who are teaching German in our nation's schools. It is important that the teaching of German not be confined in the future to a select number of large high schools where one can count on strong enrollments, that German classes also be offered in most of the middle schools and even in the elementary schools. Those of us in higher education should be thinking of ways to ensure that this happens; otherwise, I fear that German may be choked out of the curriculum by other languages that are thought to be more important or fashionable (such as Spanish, French, and even Japanese). If this happens, and there are signs that it is already happening, fewer and fewer students will be entering college with a background and an interest in German, and this has obvious implications for Germanistik as a discipline.

German Studies at the college level must become more relevant, more meaningful to those students whose primary academic interest lies in another discipline—e.g., business, engineering, international relations, etc. It no longer makes sense to design undergraduate programs aimed mainly at satisfying the needs of traditional German majors, for their number has been declining and will continue to do so in the coming years. In addition, basic language instruction in German must be outstanding and encouraging, so that undergraduates will choose to continue taking the German courses offered at more advanced levels. Far too many of today's German professors are concerned mainly with the advanced undergraduate courses in literature, and some of them are interested only in teaching graduate students. These Germanists have lost contact with students working at the base of the instructional pyramid, and also lost sight of their needs, a situation that has already had serious consequences for the discipline.

This brings me to the third and final level of concern, the nature and focus of our graduate programs in German. There are probably too many graduate programs in the United States today, and too few of them are truly of high quality. In addition, and partly due to the situation described above, there are not enough students from institutions within the United States to sustain the existing graduate programs. Many graduate programs have "solved" this problem by recruiting their graduate students from universities in Germany. Since teaching jobs are scarce in Germany, and since our graduate programs are often able to offer substantial financial support to at least their best graduate students, many German-born and German educated Germanists are understandably eager to continue their studies, cost-free, in the United States. After a few years, with the PhD in hand, many of them are prepared to compete with American-born Germanists for a limited number of teaching jobs in higher education. And, like many of the American-born Germanists, they often have little interest in teaching the lower-level German language courses to undergraduates and no interest whatever in working with those persons teaching German in the schools. They are interested primarily in teaching advanced students, preferably graduate students, and in carrying out the research projects that will lead to promotion and professional success. There is nothing wrong with this, of course, but it does not really help to further the cause of German and German Studies in the United States.

To summarize, I think we need to refocus our discipline at the college/university level, keeping in mind the educational goals and interests of today's undergraduate students; we need to reduce the number of doctoral programs and, during this process, reconsider the purpose and nature of graduate education in German; we also need to establish (I wish I could say restore) a healthier balance between German Studies at the most advanced and the most elementary levels. If we in the profession fail to take action on all these fronts, if we fail to address the problems I have only begun to outline, the discipline we know as Germanistik will most assuredly not thrive, and it may not even survive, on United States soil.

Afterthoughts

In retrospect, I think my expectations of the symposium were rather unrealistic. The patterns of thinking and behavior that we Germanists have developed over decades are difficult to change, a fact that became increasingly clear to me during the three days of discussion and deliberation at Vanderbilt. Right from the outset, I sensed a reluctance on the part of many participants to admit that there was a crisis of any dimension in the profession. This "denial" made it difficult for us to focus on the problems we are currently experiencing in Germanics from K-PhD and beyond (i.e., in the job market); consequently, it was not possible for us to begin seeking solutions to these problems. In the final session, however, the group was able to formulate an "action agenda" which appeared in the Winter 1995 AATG *Newsletter* (Vol. 30, No. 2).

The AATG's publication of the action agenda (based on written responses by Heidi Byrnes, A. Leslie Willson, and the protocol of the final session) along with a report on the Vanderbilt symposium (prepared by John McCarthy) was an extremely important next step, as it brought our concerns to the attention of everyone in the profession. All of us are indebted to Helene Zimmer-Loew, the Executive Director of the AATG, who recommended this and some other practical ways to continue the discourse on the issues raised in Nashville.

Despite my initial disappointment, I am encouraged by several things that have occured in the wake of the Vanderbilt conference. First, the large attendance and lively debate at the two follow-up forums John McCarthy and I organized for the 1995 AATG Meeting at Stanford University last August: "On the Future of German in the Schools" and "On the Future of German at the College and University Level." Second, the continuation of these forums at the AATG Meeting in Anaheim this November, to be followed next year by two more special sessions that will be held in the Midwest and on the East Coast. And third, the communications we received following the Stanford AATG Meeting from some professors who are prominent in the profession, signalling their willingness to discuss and deal with the problems confronting American Germanics.

There has been forward momentum since the symposium, and the discourse that began at Vanderbilt has continued and broadened so as to include many more members of the profession. But, as German programs are eliminated in many of our nation's schools, as undergraduate enrollments in German decline, and as budget cuts and the tight job market make other types of graduate study more attractive to this country's brightest students, there is an urgent need for immediate action even while the discussion and debate continue.

I propose therefore that everyone who teaches German at the post-secondary level in the United States do the following in 1996:

- *Inform yourself!* Find out what has happened to German at the pre-collegiate level in your community and state. (At which grade levels is it being taught? What are the enrollments? Has it been eliminated in some schools and school districts?)
- *Get involved!* Become an active advocate for the teaching of German in grades 7-12 and earlier (K-12 is our ultimate goal).
- *Reach out!* Meet with all the teachers of German in your local public and private schools and forge an alliance with them.

If each one of us is willing to become PERSONALLY involved in this manner, rather than relegating such an important responsibility to the AATG or to colleagues involved in teacher training (what might be called the United Way approach to solving our problems), we will have taken a major step together toward ensuring the vitality of our profession in the next century.

20

An Action Agenda for
German Studies in the 21st Century

HEIDI BYRNES
Georgetown University

Locate German Studies in U.S. Public Education, K–Graduate School

- Broaden the potential student population whom German Studies might serve by recognizing that our content pertains to all disciplines.
- Explore the historical role and define an appropriate position for German Studies in the contemporary context of public education in the U.S.
- Explore the possibilities of culture studies serving as an entry into the center of the U.S. curriculum.
- Create articulated sequences of instruction for language from K–12.
- Clarify the relationship between (e.g., sequence, hierarchy of access) between instructional content (e.g. culture studies) and knowledge/acquisition/teaching of German.
- Where appropriate, relate German Studies to heritage studies.
- Attract students for German Studies from minority student population.
- Devise strategies that facilitate German Studies even in an environment of resource constraints (consider local, regional,

state initiatives, constraints, opportunities).
- Present German Studies to the public more effectively, through lobbying, through translation and publishing of major works written in German, through accessing the educated public, not only internal academic groups.

Position German Studies within American Higher Education

- Consider the contribution of different graduate programs in German Studies in the country (e.g., financial viability, responsiveness to needs for future members in the profession, different intellectual emphases and student populations, job placement).
- Relate culture studies and multiculturalism to the place and role of German Studies.
- Develop a cadre of effective leaders in German Studies and/or in foreign language departments.
- Offer German Studies programs at the graduate level that recognize and use to greatest advantage graduate students' highly varied undergraduate majors.

Define the Intellectual Center, Mission, and Goals of German Studies and Translate This into Curricula

- Identify and strengthen our intellectual core before establishing alliances across the disciplines.
- Bridge the gap between language instruction and instruction in academic content (e.g., literature, culture, linguistics).
- Emphasize the contributions to current intellectual debates that arise from the German-speaking world (e.g., Nietzsche, Adorno, Heidegger).
- Devise strategies for making German Studies available to the broadest possible audience.
- Coordinate lower- and upper-division classes in the undergraduate curriculum.

Educate and Develop a German Profession
That Is Able To Carry Out This Future Agenda

• Develop a professional culture which upholds a professional ethos that focuses on the public welfare (society at large, our students in particular), and the welfare of *all* members of the profession, regardless of educational level and academic specialization.

• Continue discussions in national and regional meetings.

• Create networks for monitoring and developing members of the profession.

• Offer support services and outreach from higher education to the schools.

• Explore career opportunities for graduate students beyond the academy.

• Bridge the gap between language instruction and academic content.

• Reconsider requirements for hiring and tenuring of faculty.

• Increase minority faculty representation.

LIST OF PARTICIPANTS

DAAD CONFERENCE
October 13–16, 1994

1. David Benseler, Chair and Prof. of German, Case Western Reserve Univ.
2. Jane Brown, Prof. of German & Comparative Lit., Univ. of Washington
3. Keith Bullivant, Chair & Prof. of German, Univ. of Florida
4. Heidi Byrnes, Prof. of German, Georgetown Univ.
5. Sara Friedrichsmeyer, Prof. of German, Univ. of Cincinnati
6. Gerald Gillespie, Prof. of German & Comp. Lit., Stanford Univ.
7. Ülker Göckberk, Chair and Assoc. Prof. of German, Reed College
8. Diane Harper, Assoc. Prof. of German, Middle Tennessee State Univ.
9. Claudia Hahn-Raabe, Dir. of Language Programs, Goethe House NY
10. Alice C. Harris, Chair, Department of Germanic and Slavic Langs.
11. Sonja Hedgepeth, Assoc. Prof. of German, Middle Tennessee State Univ.
12. Patricia Herminghouse, Prof. of German, Univ. of Rochester
13. Peter Uwe Hohendahl, Prof. of German, Cornell Univ.
14. Donald Holman, Ph.D. candidate in Comparative Literature at Vanderbilt Univ.
15. Robert Holub, Chair & Prof. of German, UC-Berkeley
16. Dieter Jedan, Chair & Prof. of German, Southeast Missouri State Univ.
17. Doris Kirchner, Assistant Prof. of German, Univ. of Rhode Island
18. Wilfried Krug, German Embassy, Washington DC
19. Alice A. Kuzniar, Assoc. Prof. of German, Univ. of North Carolina

20. James K. Lyon, Prof. of German, Brigham Young Univ.
21. Amy Marshall, Assistant Prof. of German, Univ. of Alabama
22. John A. McCarthy, Prof. of German & Comp. Lit., Vanderbilt Univ.
23. Joseph McVeigh, Chair & Assoc. Prof. of German, Smith College
24. Jennifer Michaels, Chair and Prof. of German, Grinnell College
25. Wolfgang Natter, Assoc. Prof. of German, Univ. of Kentucky
26. Valters Nollendorfs, Prof. of German, Univ. of Wisconsin
27. Thomas P. Saine, Prof. of German, UC-Irvine
28. Katrin Schneider, Ph.D. candidate in German Vanderbilt Univ.
29. Renate Schulz, Prof. of German, Univ. of Arizona
30. Dieter Sevin, Professor of German
31. Leigh Stahl, Ph.D. candidate in German, Vanderbilt Univ.
32. Heidrun Suhr, Director, DAAD NY
33. Lynne Tatlock, Chair & Prof. of German, Washington Univ.
34. Frank Trommler, Prof. of German & Comp. Literature, Penn
35. John Van Cleve, Prof. of German, Mississippi State Univ.
36. Marc A. Weiner, Assoc. Prof. of German, Indiana Univ.
37. A. Leslie Willson, Prof. emer. of German, Univ. of Texas-Austin
38. Helene Zimmer-Lowe, Executive Director, AATG
39. Richard A. Zipser, Chair & Prof. of German, Univ. of Delaware

VANDERBILT SYMPOSIUM PROGRAM

DAAD CONFERENCE ON:

"Germanistik in the USA: Prospects for Change—Changing Our Prospects"

October 13-16, 1994
Vanderbilt University, Nashville Tennessee
All meetings will take place in 118 Sarrat Student Center

PROGRAM

Day 1: Thursday, October 13, 1994

Afternoon   Arrival of Participants
               Hotel, The Hampton Inn at Vanderbilt University
6:30-8:00 PM   Reception in the Lobby of Kirkland Hall
               Hosted by Joe B. Wyatt, Chancellor of Vanderbilt U

Day 2: Friday, October 14, 1994

9:00 AM   WELCOME AND INTRODUCTION:

               Moderator: John A. McCarthy, Vanderbilt U
               Thomas Burish, Provost, Vanderbilt U
               Madeleine J. Goodman, Dean, College of Arts &
               Science, Vanderbilt U
               Heidrun Suhr, Director, DAAD, New York Office

9:30 AM   DEFINING THE PROBLEM—
               SETTING THE PARAMETERS

               Moderator: Richard A. Zipser, U of Delaware

	John A. McCarthy, Vanderbilt U
	"Double Optics: The Americanization of Germanistik — The Germanizing of Americans"
9:50 AM	John Van Cleve, Mississippi State U
	A. Leslie Willson, U of Texas at Austin
	"Reform or Retreat: Whither American Germanics"
10:15 AM	Discussion
10:45 AM	Coffee Break
11:15 AM	Peter Uwe Hohendahl
	"The American-German Divide"
11:35 AM	Comment: Lynne Tatlock, Washington U
11:45 AM	Discussion
12:30 PM	Lunch

2:00 PM	OUR PROFESSIONAL PROFILE
	Moderator: Helene Zimmer-Loew, AATG

2:00 PM	Renate A. Schulz, U of Arizona
	"The Profile of our Profession"
2:15 PM	David Benseler, Case Western Reserve U
	"Language Training and the Job Market"
2:30 PM	Robert Holub, UC-Berkeley
	"Graduate Education in German: Past Experience and Future Perspectives"
2:45 PM	Discussion
3:30 PM	Coffee Break

4:00 PM	VISIBILITY IN THE ACADEMY: POSITIONINGS
	Moderator: Jane Brown, U of Washington

4:00 PM	Heidi Byrnes, Georgetown U
	"How Visible Are We Now?"
4:15 PM	James Lyon, Brigham Young U
	"The Limits of Exposure"
4:30 PM	Comment: Richard Zipser, U of Delaware

4:40 PM	Discussion
5:30 PM	Adjourn
6:30 PM	Reception, Hosted by Department of
	Germanic & Slavic Languages, Vanderbilt U
	Location: Robert Penn Warren
	Humanities Ctr, Vaughn Home
8:00 PM	Dinner at Sfuzzi (group function)

Day 3: Saturday, October 15, 1994

9:30 AM   TOWARD THE AMERICANIZATION OF THE
UNDERGRADUATE CURRICULUM

Moderator: Jennifer Michaels, Grinnell College

Joseph McVeigh, Smith College
*"The Undergraduate Curriculum:
What's Right / Wrong With It?"*

9:45 AM   Dieter Jedan, Southeast Missouri State U
"Reshaping the Undergraduate Experience"

10:00 AM   Comment: Doris Kirchner, U of Rhode Island

10:10 AM   Comment: John Van Cleve, Mississippi State U

10:20 AM   Discussion

11:00 AM   Coffee Break

11:15 AM   TOWARD THE AMERICANIZATION OF
THE GRADUATE CURRICULUM

Moderator: Dieter Sevin, Vanderbilt U

Gerald Gillespie, Stanford U
*"The Graduate Curriculum:
What's Right / Wrong With It?"*

11:30 AM   Jane Brown, U of Washington
*"The Graduate Curriculum:
What's Right / Wrong With It?"*

11:45 AM   Keith Bullivant, U of Florida
            "The Graduate Curriculum:
            What's Right/Wrong With It?"
12:00 PM   Discussion
12:30 PM   Lunch

2:00 PM   (RE)SHAPING THE PROFESSION
            THROUGH MULTIPERSPECTIVISM

            Moderator: Patricia Herminghouse, U of Rochester

2:00 PM   Alice A. Kuzniar, U of North Carolina at Chapel Hill
            "Cross-Gendered Cross-Cultural Studies
            and the German Program"
2:15 PM   Frank Trommler, U of Pennsylvania
            "Everyman his own Cultural Historian"
2:30 PM   Comment: Wolfgang Natter, U of Kentucky
            Ülker Gökberk, Reed College
2:45 PM   Discussion
3:30 PM   Coffee Break

3:45 PM   (RE)SHAPING THE PROFESSION
            THROUGH PUBLISHING:

            A PANEL DISCUSSION

            Moderator: James Lyon, Brigham Young U

            David Benseler, Case Western Reserve U
                (Modern Language Journal)
            Sara Friedrichsmeyer, U of Cincinnati
                (Women in German Yearbook)
            Thomas Saine, UC-Irvine
                (Goethe Yearbook)
            Marc Weiner, U of Indiana
                (German Quarterly)
            Peter Uwe Hohendahl, Cornell U

(*New German Critique*)
A. Leslie Willson, U of Texas at Austin
(*Dimension*)
4:45 PM   Open Forum
5:30 PM   Adjourn
6:00 PM   Reception, Hosted by the
             U of Delaware at The University Club
7:30 PM   Dinner at the Wild Horse Saloon (group function)

Day 4: Sunday, October 16, 1994

9:15 AM   AN ACTION AGENDA FOR THE 21ST CENTURY

             Moderator: John A. McCarthy. Vanderbilt U

             FACULTY PERSPECTIVE
             Sara Friedrichsmeyer, U of Cincinnati
             Ülker Gökberk, Reed College
             Patricia Herminghouse, U of Rochester
             Doris Kirchner, U of Rhode Island
             Wolfgang Natter, U of Kentucky
             Thomas P. Saine, UC-Irvine
             Lynne Tatlock, Washington U
             Frank Trommler, U of Pennsylvania
             Richard A. Zipser, U of Delaware

10:15 AM   "A Graduate-Student Perspective"
             Don Holman, Katrin Schneider, Leigh Stahl,
             Vanderbilt U

10:30 AM   OPEN FORUM

11:00 AM   CONCLUDING REMARKS

             Wilfried Krug, German Embassy
             John A. McCarthy & Richard A. Zipser
11:30 AM   Farewell

This conference is made possible by the generous support of the DAAD and the following units of Vanderbilt University: Office of the Provost, College of Arts and Science, Graduate School, Department of Germanic & Slavic Languages, and the Center for European Studies. Additionally, funds were provided by the Department of Foreign Languages & Literatures at the University of Delaware.

REQUIRED READING:

John Van Cleve and A. Leslie Willson. *Remarks on the Needed Reform of German Studies in the USA*. Columbia SC: Camden House, 1993.

RECOMMENDED READINGS:

D. Benseler, "The Upper-Division Curriculum in FL & Literatures: Obstacles to the Realization of Promise." In: *Critical Issues in Foreign-Language Instruction*. Ed. Ellen S. Silber. New York: Garland, 1991. 186-99.

Willi Goetschel, "Germanistik in den USA," *Weimarer Beiträge* 39.3 (1993): 325-43.

Uwe P. Hohendahl, "Interdisciplinary German Studies: Tentative Conclusions," *The German Quarterly* 62.2 (Spring 1989): 227-34.

Valters Nollendorfs, "Out of *Germanistik*: Thoughts on the Shape of Things to Come," *Der Unterrichtspraxis* 27.1 (1994): 1-10.

R. Schultz, "Profile of our Profession," *Der Unterrichtspraxis* 26.2 (Fall 1993): 229-52.

F. Trommler (ed.). *Germanistik in den USA. Neue Entwicklungen und Methoden*. Opladen: Westdeutscher Verlag, 1989.

F. Trommler, "Einleitung," 7-43.

W. Koepke, "Germanistik als eine deutsche-amerikanische Wissenschaft," 46-65.

H. J. Schmidt, "Wissenschaft als Ware und als Selbstbehauptung. Die institutionellen Grundlagen der amerikanischen Germanistik," 66-81.

J. Sammons, "Germanistik in Niemandsland," 104-120.

F. Trommler, Michael Geyer, and Jeffrey Peck. "Germany as the Other: Towards an American Agenda for German Studies, A Colloquium." *German Studies Review* 13 (1990): 111-38.

BIBLIOGRAPHY

Those entries marked with an asterix (*) were recommended reading in preparation for the Vanderbilt symposium.

Ansichten einer künftigen Germanistik. Edited by Jürgen Kolbe. München: Hanser, 1969.

Becker, Carl. *Everyman His Own Historian: Essays on History and Politics.* Chicago: U of Chicago P, 1966.

*Benseler, David P. "The Upper-Division Curriculum in Foreign Languages and Literatures: Obstacles to the Realization of Promise." In: *Critical Issues in Foreign Language Instruction.* Ed. Ellen S. Silber. New York: Garland, 1991. 186-99.

Bowen, William G., and Julie Ann Sosa. *Prospects for Faculty in the Arts and Sciences: A Study of Factors Affecting Demand and Supply, 1987-2012.* Princeton: Princeton U P, 1989.

Butler, Judith. *Bodies that Matter: On the Discursive Limits of "Sex."* New York: Routledge, 1993.

Challenges of Germanistik: Traditions and Prospects of an Academic Discipline = Germanistik Weltweit?: Zur Theorie und Praxis des Disziplinrahmens. Ed. by Eitel Timm. München: Iudicium, 1992.

German Studies in the United States: Assessment and Outlook. Edited by Walter F. W. Lohnes & Valters Nollendorfs. Madison WI: U of Wisconsin P, 1976.

Germanistik as German Studies: Interdisciplinary Theories and Methods. Special Issue of *The German Quarterly* 62.2 (1989)

Germanistik—Eine Deutsche Wissenschaft. Beiträge von E. Lämmert, W. Killy, K. O. Conrady and P. V. Polenz. Frankfurt a.M.: Suhrkamp, 1967.

Germanistik in den USA. Special issue of *Weimarer Beiträge* 39.3 (1993). Ed. by Willi Goetschel.

Germanistik in den USA. Neue Entwicklungen und Methoden. Ed. by Frank Trommler. Opladen: Westdeutscher Verlag, 1989.

Gillespie, Gerald. "Home Truths and Institutional Falsehoods." In: *Building a Profession: Autobiographical Perspectives on the Beginnings of Comparative Literature in the United States.* Ed. by Lionel Gossman and Mihai I, Spariosu. Albany: State University of New York Press, 1994. 159-175.

———. "Rhinoceros, Unicorn, or Chimera?—A Polysystemic View of Possible Kinds of Comparative Literature in the New Century." *Journal of Intercultural Studies* 19 (1992): 14-21.

———. "Comparative Literature of the 1990s in the U.S.A." In: *Issues and Methods in Comparative Studies.* Ed. by Tania Franco Carvalhal. (forthcoming)

*Goetschel, Willi. "Zu diesem Heft: *Germanistik in den USA.*" *Weimarer Beiträge* 39.3 (1993): 325-43.

Höyng, Peter. "Zur 'Krise' der Germanistik in den USA," *Zeitschrift für Literaturwissenschaft und Linguistik* 97 (1995): 162-65.

*Hohendahl, Peter U. "Interdisciplinary German Studies: Tentative Conclusions." *The German Quarterly* 62.2 (1989): 227-34.

Huber, Bettina J. et al. "Annex No. 8: Report on the Job Information Service" (ms. presented to the MLA Executive Council Meeting 25-26 February 1994).

Hunt, Lynn. "The Virtues of Disciplinarity." *Eighteenth-Century Studies* 28 (1994): 1-7.

Interkulturelle Germanistik: Dialog der Kulturen auf Deutsch? Ed. by Peter Zimmermann. 2nd rev. ed. Frankfurt a/M: Peter Lang, 1991.

*Koepke, Wulf. "Germanistik als eine deutsch-amerikanische Wissenschaft." In: *Germanistik in den USA: Neue Entwicklungen und Methoden.* Ed. by Frank Trommler. Opladen: Westdeutscher Verlag, 1989. 46-65.

Lange, Victor. "Thoughts in Season." In: *German Studies in the United States: Assessment and Outlook.* Ed. by Walter F. W. Lohnes and Valters Nollendorfs. Madison WI: U of Wisconsin P, 1976. 5-16.

———. "The History of German Studies in America: Ends and Means." In: *Teaching German in America. Prolegomena to a History.* Ed. by David P. Benseler, Walter F. W. Lohnes, & Valters Nollendorfs. Madison WI: U of Wisconsin P, 1988. 3-14.

Lively, Kit. "State Support for Public Colleges Up 2% This Year." *Chronicle of Higher Education* (27 October 1993): A29, A32-A34.

Magner, Denise K. "Many Colleges Have Survived by Moving Away From the Liberal Arts, Author of New Book Says." *Chronicle of Higher Education* (2 March 1994): A18.

Martin, Biddy. "Zwischenbilanz der feministischen Debatten." In: *Germanistik in den USA: Neue Entwicklungen und Methoden.* Ed. by Frank Trommler. Opladen: Westdeutscher Verlag, 1989. 165-95.

Mueller, Martin. "Yellow Stripes and Dead Amarillos." *Profession 89* (1989): 23-31.

Neue Ansichten einer künftigen Germanistik. Ed. by Jürgen Kolbe. München: Hanser, 1974.

Nollendorfs, Valters, and Geofrrey S. Koby. *Directory of German Studies: Departments, Programs, and Faculties in the United States and Canada 1990.* New York: German Studies Information Limited, 1991.

————."Eine amerikanischere Germanistik. Entwicklungen im amerikanischen Deutschstudium in den 70er und 80er Jahren." *Zeitschrift für Kulturaustausch* 35 (1985): 230-36.

*————. "Out of *Germanistik*: Thoughts on the Shape of Things to Come." *Die Unterrichtspraxis* 27.1 (1994): 1-10.

Peck, Jeffrey. "There's No Place Like Home? Remapping the Topography of German Studies." *The German Quarterly* 62.2 (1989): 178-89.

"Personalia 1987/88." *Monatshefte* 79.3 (1987): 320-66.

Rethinking "Germanistik": Canon and Culture. Ed. by Robert Bledsoe, Bernd Estabrook, J. Courtney Federle, Kay Henschel, Wayne Miller, & Arnim Polster. New York: Peter Lang, 1991.

*Sammons, Jeffrey. "Germanistik in Niemandsland." In: *Germanistik in den USA. Neue Entwicklungen und Methoden.* Ed. by Frank Trommler. Opladen: Westdeutscher Verlag, 1989. 104-20;

————. "Some Considerations on Our Invisibility," In: *German Studies in the United States: Assessment and Outlook.* Ed. by Walter F. W. Lohnes and Valters Nollendorfs. Madison WI: U Wisconsin P, 1976. 17-23.

*Schmidt, Henry J. "Wissenschaft als Ware und als Selbstbehauptung. Die institutionellen Grundlagen der amerikanischen Germanistik." In: *Germanistik in den USA. Neue Entwicklungen und Methoden*. Ed. by Frank Trommler. Opladen: Westdeutscher Verlag, 1989. 66-83.

*Schulz, Renate. "Profile of our Profession." *Der Unterrichtspraxis* 26.2 (1993): 229-52.

Sibley Fries, Marilyn. "Rezeption deutschsprachiger Autorinnen in den USA." *Weimarer Beiträge* 39.3 (1993): 410-46.

Steinfeld, Thomas et al. "Germanistik—disziplinäre Identität und kulturelle Leistung." *Frankfurter Allgemeine Zeitung*, Mittwoch, 7. September 1994, Nr. 208, Seite N5.

Suhr, Heidrun. "German Studies in North America: Contexts and Perspectives." In: *Präludien. Kanadisch-Deutsche Dialoge*. Ed. Burkhardt Krause, Ulrich Scheck, and Patrick O'Neill. München: Judicium Verlag, 1992. 105-119.

Teaching German in America: Prolegomena to a History. Edited by David P. Benseler, Walter F. W. Lohnes, & Valters Nollendorfs. Madison WI: U of Wisconsin P, 1988.

*Trommler, Frank. "Einleitung." In: *Germanistik in den USA: Neue Entwicklungen und Methoden*. Ed. by Frank Trommler. Opladen: Westdeutscher Verlag, 1989. 7-42.

———. "The Future of German Studies or How to Define Interdisciplinarity in the 1990s." *German Studies Review* 15 (1992): 201-17.

———. "Über die Lesbarkeit der deutschen Literatur." In: *Germanistik in den USA. Neue Entwicklungen und Methoden*. Ed. by Frank Trommler. Opladen: Westdeutscher Verlag, 1989. 222-259.

———. Michael Geyer, & Jeffrey Peck. "Germany as the Other: Towards an American Agenda for German Studies, A Colloquium." *German Studies Review* 13 (1990): 111-38.

*Van Cleve, John and A. Leslie Willson. *Remarks on the Needed Reform of German Studies in the United States*. Columbia SC: Camden House, 1993.

Wozu noch Germanistik? Wissenschaft, Beruf, Kulturelle Praxis. Ed. by Jürgen Förster, Eva Neuland, & Gerhard Rupp. Stuttgart: Metzler, 1989.

Zammito, John H. "Are We Being Theoretical Yet? The New Historicism, the New Philosophy of History, and 'Practicing Historians.'" *Journal of Modern History* 65 (1993): 786.

www.ingramcontent.com/pod-product-compliance
Lightning Source LLC
Chambersburg PA
CBHW030651270326
41929CB00007B/307